ABUNDANT LIVING

Finding Peace, Purpose, Passion and Provision

Zoe M. Hicks

For Becky –
Truly one of my oldest friends!
God loves you
and so do I!
Zoe

Lighthouse Press, Inc.

Lighthouse Press, Inc.
1907 Mercedes Ct.
Atlanta, GA 30345
Phone: 404-633-1310

First published by Lighthouse Press October 1, 2009.

ISBN 10: 0-615-31493-7
ISBN 13: 978-0-615-31493-8
Library of Congress Control Number: 2009908237

Printed in the United States of America
Atlanta, Georgia

Scripture quotations are from The Amplified® Bible, ©1965 by the Lockman Foundation, used by permission (www.lockman.org)

For

Alice Catherine Hicks,

precious daughter and loyal friend.

TABLE OF CONTENTS

GOD'S PROVISION

1   The Abundant Life   11
2   An Abundance of Purpose   21
3   An Abundance of Mentors   31
4   An Abundance of Prosperity   41
5   An Abundance of Progress   51
6   An Abundance of Healings   59
7   An Abundance of Deliverance   69
8   An Abundant Inheritance   79

CHARACTER TRAITS FOR ABUNDANT LIVING

9   An Abundance of an Awareness of
   God's Presence   89
10   An Abundance of Dependence on God   99
11   An Abundance of Persistence   109
12   An Abundance of Inner Peace   117
13   An Abundance of Gratitude   127
14   An Abundance of Joy   137
   End Notes   144

Introduction and Acknowledgments

I have always been puzzled by dear Christian friends who never seem to me to be happy. They may have everything in their lives going well for them except for one problem. Yet, all they can think about is their problem. As I listen to them talk, I think "but you are so talented (or rich, or healthy, or successful, or blessed with friends and family, or smart (and the list goes on and on)). I want them to appreciate all that they *do* have and the incredible God that can help them with their one little problem.

To the secular world, abundant living means the big house in a prestigious neighborhood, a vacation home getaway, a fancy new car, the right job, the right friends, good health and power or influence. There is nothing wrong with these things provided we keep them in perspective. If we don't, they will prevent us from living the truly abundant life. Jesus said, "I am come that you might have life and have it in all of its abundance." What exactly does that mean? I believe it means appreciating all the big and little things He does for us every day, recognizing all the deliverances, provisions, guidance, comfort, rest, peace, progress, mentors, eternal life, and encouragement He sends. How can we not live abundantly if we open our eyes to all He has provided?

In many ways we are blind. We need to wake up and live like we are children of the King. We are princes and princesses, here on a royal mission. We need to start acting like it because there are many desperate people out there. If we can learn to recognize and receive abundance from our Father, the King, we can use it to help and bless ourselves, our loved ones and many others.

I am grateful to so many people who have helped me with this book. The teenagers at Oak Grove United Methodist Church, Decatur, Georgia, provided insight for the chapter on mentors; Virginia Sowell designed the beautiful cover; Michelle Gibbons faithfully transcribed my messy writing into neatly typed pages; Marylou Barry edited my grammar and punctuation; my incredible Bible study group prayed for the writing of this book and forgave me when I skipped meetings to write; my wonderful husband kept giving me those "Attagirls" he's so good about, and so many friends and readers encouraged me and told me to keep writing. I love you all.

I pray this book will open your eyes to the abundance we have as God's children. And, being aware, I hope you will move forward with your God given dreams.

Remember – you are never alone. Live abundantly!

Zoe. M. Hicks

GOD'S PROVISION

Chapter 1

THE ABUNDANT LIFE

*L*et's imagine ourselves the heroes or heroines of an exciting adventure story. We are about to leave our ordinary worlds (perhaps even reluctantly) and embark on a journey which may be physical, spiritual, or psychological. There will be problems, tests, and challenges along the way. Hostile forces must be overcome and sacrifices made but, by leaving the worlds we know and entering the special adventure world, we will most certainly be transformed through our experience and acquire wisdom, knowledge, and character traits we did not previously possess. Once acquired, these new gifts can be taken back to our ordinary worlds and used to bless and transform the people we love.

Fortunately, we will not have to do this alone, because it would not be possible. The hostile forces are too powerful, the obstacles too great.

Although we will feel totally inadequate and completely overwhelmed at times, God is with us on our special adventures. He does not want us to continue in our ho-hum existences, just treading water or getting by. He wants us to step out and reach for what He has put in our hearts, trusting

Him for the strength and wisdom to accomplish His purposes in and through us.

Not everyone we know will be happy about our decisions to leave the status quo. Adversaries (perhaps even in our own families) will appear and dark forces will oppose us as we travel our God-given paths, but one thing will be certain: We will no longer be living dull lives. Every day will bring new challenges and new rewards. We will get to see God working as we never have before.

God intends for us to live abundantly.

God will not force us to overcome the obstacles and be the hero or heroine He intends, because in His infinite goodness He gives us free choice. But He will, as all good parents sometimes have to do, push us out of our comfort zone nest so we will learn to fly.

If we are going to live abundantly, we have to stay the course He charts for us, remain very close to Him, and lean on Him for our purpose, provision, strength, wisdom, guidance, deliverance, and security. This is God's best for us. He intended for us to live abundantly. He sent His Son not only to save us by paying the penalty for our sins, but that we might have life in all of its abundance, "to the full, till it overflows."[1]

The purpose of this book is to help and encourage us to do that. First, we'll look at seven areas in which God has made provision for us so that we can live abundantly: Purpose, Mentors, Prosperity, Progress, Healings, Deliverance, and Inheritance. Then we'll look at character traits we need to live abundantly and that abundant living develops in us: Awareness of God's Presence, Dependence on Him, Persistence, Peace, Gratitude, and Joy.

As we begin to live abundantly, and as these character traits manifest in our lives, people will notice. Just by letting God have His way (which is always better than ours), we will draw people to the Good Shepherd.

Each of us will have a different journey, our own unique adventure. Our adversaries will be different. For one of us it might be internal; for another, an external foe to defeat. Our vocations will be tailored to the special gifts and talents God has given us, although our purpose will be the same, as we will see.

GOD'S PROVISION

Purpose

To live abundantly we need to know we have a reason for being here. But, what is it? Do I have a different purpose than you?

Once we belong to God through His Son, our purpose, in a nutshell, is to glorify Him and live so that others will come to Him and be blessed. But, because we are all so different, we will find as many ways to do that as there are numbers of us. God does care *how* we do that, and even as He sends mentors, He sends guidance (which takes many different forms) to show us when we're on the right path and when we're not.

If I had thought I would (as a young woman, that is) be able to glorify God through my athletic abilities, God would have quickly shown me, through one athletic disaster after another, that I needed to look around for another direction. I specifically remember knocking the light fixture down in the college gym as I was serving for my volleyball team. The coach came over, rolled her eyes and shook her head. But I did get encouragement in the classroom. *I get it, God. Forget athletics. Focus on academics.*

Mentors

The word mentor comes to us from Homer's *The Odyssey*,

after a character who guides the hero on his journey.[2] Mentors are God's gift to us on our journey – wiser, nobler people who impart their experiences and wisdom to us at strategic points along the way. A mentor can also serve as our sounding board, motivator, or informant.

Some of our mentors will be close – parents, grandparents, and teachers for example. Some will be virtual – authors, actors, directors, artists that we will never meet but who will encourage and inspire us through their work.

Some may give us a physical gift (Luke Skywalker's mentor gave him his father's lightsaber); others will give us their time, talents, and wisdom to help us on our journey. Mordecai, Queen Esther's uncle and mentor, gave her wise counsel.

Some will just appear in our lives, but others we will have to seek out. All are God's gift to us. And, if we live long enough, we in turn must seek ways to mentor those coming behind us. It may become our primary mission at some point in our life.

Prosperity

Prosperity here means having adequate resources to do exactly what God has called us to do. He called George Müller to build orphanages in England. At the time he was called he had only two coins in his pocket, but God miraculously sent over $7 million to build and maintain the buildings Mr. Müller would need to care for over 2,000 orphans. During the 60 years Mr. Müller had charge of the orphans, they never missed a meal. God provided. Müller had the prosperity he needed to fulfill his calling.

Some people are gifted to earn extraordinary sums of money, and because of their gift they are expected to give extraordinary sums to God's work. Maybe God will move one or more of these people to finance your calling.

As we step out into our great adventure following God, we should take comfort in the fact that God's work will always have God's resources to continue. After all, God owns it all, and He can shift it where and when it's needed.

Progress

"God is not through with me yet," someone wrote. As long as we are here (and maybe in heaven, too) God wants us to grow and mature spiritually as well as in other ways. If a teacher saw his or her student stagnating, not making progress, the teacher would have the student repeat the lesson or grade until the needed level of mastery was achieved. It would not be acceptable for the student to remain at the same level. Certainly we find great joy in becoming more and more skilled at a particular task, and God wants us to find joy as we are able to love Him more completely and imitate Him more perfectly. He also wants us to find great satisfaction as we gain skill and expertise in whatever we are doing. Progress is the law of the Kingdom.

Healings

Health is a tremendous asset in our quest to live abundantly. To live a healthy life we will need to practice those good health habits we have been taught. But we will also need to be healed, if not in our bodies, then in some area of our lives. Something, sooner or later, is going to get "sick." By learning to receive healing, wherever it might hurt, we can quickly move back into abundant living.

Deliverances

On our exciting adventure we will encounter opposition. If

we are called to do something great for God (I believe we all are), dark forces will try to stop us. "Deliver us from evil," Jesus taught us to pray, and we will need to be delivered. The Bible is full of stories of supernatural, miraculous deliverances. Remember the Israelite children, facing the Red Sea to their front with Pharoah and the Egyptian army closing in? They had no time to build boats to cross. God just parted the waters for them to *walk* across. When Pharoah and *his* army tried that, in hot pursuit, the water closed in on them, resulting in a complete annihilation. What did the Israelites do? They trusted. Moses stretched out his hands and the waters parted.

We'll need to be delivered many times from many adversaries and hindrances in the course of our adventure. Sometimes we'll need deliverance from lack, sometimes from attack on our ministry or reputation, sometimes from our own stupidity. But we'll surely need it and God will provide.

Inheritance

We all have a great inheritance in the here and now. Anyone who reads can tap into the great writers and thinkers by going to a public library. We are beneficiaries of all who have gone before. Their work protects us (medicine), inspires us (music, art, literature, drama), makes our lives easier (science, engineering), and encourages and mentors us (biographies of great men and women of the faith).

I sometimes think of how many people pray for cures to some of our most feared diseases, cancer for example. A cure will come. God will work through our scientists and we will all be the beneficiaries. We will live longer and be healthier. That's part of our here and now inheritance.

But God has provided so much more – the sure knowledge He, through His Son, has dealt with all the *really* hard stuff –

16

death and sin. They have been conquered. We know the end of the story. Our entanglements with all obstacles, setbacks, and dark forces on our exciting adventure are only temporary.

CHARACTER TRAITS FOR ABUNDANT LIVING

Awareness of God's Presence

Let's say on our journey we are in a dark time, maybe under attack. Learning to become aware of God's Presence at such times will strengthen us, encourage us, and enable us to overcome. God's Presence overrides everything else. It gives us a whole new perspective and makes everything else pale by comparison.

In our crazy 21st century world, we are so busy, going a thousand miles a minute, being bombarded by messages on every side (TV, billboards, newspapers, magazines prominently displayed in stores we frequent, Internet ads), that sometimes it takes an intervening force to shake us out of our comfort zone, get our attention, and make us aware of God's Presence. Then, we find, experiencing God's Presence is the key to abundantly living. "Yes, though I walk through the [deep, sunless] valley of the shadow of death, I will fear or dread no evil, for you are with me."[3]

Dependence on God

Abundant living means we will produce fruit. Fruit, said Jesus, can be produced only when we abide (stay connected) to Him.[4]

If we don't learn to depend on God, our source, we will sooner or later fall flat on our faces.

In our society, "dependence" has gotten a bad rap. We are taught to be independent, self-supporting, hardworking, self-reliant people. But in God's economy, depending on Him is the only way we will ever be able to accomplish the mission He has set before us (our very own version of *Mission Impossible*). Dependence, then, becomes both essential and a great comfort. It's a comfort because we don't have to accomplish our mission in our own limited strength, or with our own meager resources. God's abundance is there for us.

Determination and Persistence

"Hang in there," we say, when someone is going through a tough time. And, that's good advice. If we quit every time something didn't go our way or every time something got "too hard," we'd never accomplish anything worthwhile. In short, we would not live abundantly.

James W. Moore tells the story of a sales manager trying to rev up his reps in *Healing Where It Hurts:*

"Did the Wright Brothers quit?" he yelled.
"No!" shouted the group, enthusiastically.
"Did Joan of Arc quit?" he continued.
"No!" they yelled back in one accord.
"Did Abraham Lincoln give up?"
"No, no!" they immediately responded.
"Did Thurston Marcowitz quit?" he shouted.
The group fell silent. Finally one brave soul stood up. "Sir, we have never heard of Thurston Marcowitz."
The sales manager smiled. "Of course you haven't. He quit."

Inner Peace

As we travel through this great adventure called life, we will encounter stormy weather. It's inevitable. To have inner peace regardless of the circumstances is possible only when we learn to trust God absolutely and completely.

Charles Wesley, the great hymn writer, wrote "O For a

Thousand Tongues to Sing" after observing the Moravians sailing on the same ship as he was to America. As the journey proceeded, they sailed into a fierce storm and Charles thought all was lost. The Moravians, however, in the midst of the wind, waves, and general panic, were calmly singing songs of praise to God. Despite the storm, they retained their inner peace. To have peace that passes understanding allows us to live abundantly.

Gratitude

We, of course, need to be grateful for what we're really grateful for – homes, food, family, friends, schools, and charities that have helped us and others. But we also need to learn to be grateful *period* to live abundantly. This means being grateful for the privilege of life itself and for God's continuous provision for us, whether things are going our way or not.

Gratitude adds greatly to our happiness and health, studies have shown. If we are constantly counting our blessings, we don't have time to realize we might not have as much as our neighbor. Comparisons get us in trouble unless we're comparing ourselves today with ourselves yesterday. If so, let's be grateful for the progress!

Joy

Finally, to live abundantly we need to take time for celebrations, rest, fun, and vacations. It's not at all frivolous. Without these needed times of refreshing, we would get burned out and quit. How many marriages have failed because one spouse is a workaholic? How many kids have gotten into drugs or gangs because their parents never had time to stop and just be with them, having fun, talking, visiting?

We need balance in our lives, and joy is very much a part of that.

My prayer for each of us is that when we see all God has provided for us to live abundantly, we will not hesitate to take the step of faith into the exciting world of adventure He has planned. Move over, Indiana Jones, here we come!

Chapter 2

AN ABUNDANCE OF PURPOSE

*W*hy am I here? That's a question that caused more than 22 million people to purchase a copy of Rick Warren's book, *The Purpose Driven Life*. This book made publishing history after simultaneously hitting number one on all four major bestseller lists, including the *New York Times*, *Wall Street Journal*, *USA Today*, and *Publishers Weekly*. In fact, it stayed on the *New York Times* bestseller list for a record 114 weeks.

People want more from life than just making it from one day to the next. We want to know our lives can make a difference – that we have a mission to accomplish. But what is it? How do we know what we're supposed to do?

I remember an old television series: Mission Impossible. Three "good guys" (actually one was a "good gal") would receive a tape and envelope. They would listen to the tape to learn what the mission was and then open the envelope to see the pictures of their adversaries. The tape would always include, "Your mission, if you choose to accept it ..." and would self-destruct thirty seconds after it was played. The mission would be along the lines of a James Bond assignment – a save-the-world challenge sure to entail danger, risk, intrigue, and great skill, but equally sure to bring the satisfaction of doing something *really* important and essential to the survival of the planet. Never once did the good guys and gal decline the challenge. That's what they were here for. If they died trying, so be it.

Mother Teresa, who was more realistic, said, "We cannot do great things, only small things with great love."[5] And we know *Mission Impossible* is pure fiction. Still, we want and need a purpose for living.

My husband and I belonged to a Presbyterian Church years ago. The Presbyterians have a catechism used for teaching Christian doctrine. The format is question and answer, and question number one is: What is the chief aim of man? The answer: To glorify God and enjoy Him forever. I always loved that – so simple, yet so profound. Rick Warren, had he been available to consult with the writers of the catechism, would probably have beefed it up a bit. Maybe "To love and glorify God above all, to love and lead people to Him, and to enjoy Him and fellowship with His people forever."

Beyond this, we need to figure out how and where we are uniquely called to fulfill the chief aim of man. The possibilities are endless so we do need to pray for guidance and meditate on pertinent Scriptures,[6] knowing God will surely show us if we just make ourselves available.

Pressure to Find Purpose

Katie Brazelton found herself divorced and devoid of roles that previously defined her life. The transition was agonizing. During this time, she found herself considering if the only purpose of her life she had left was shopping, or retail therapy as some call it. Katie says the lack of purpose in her life during this time almost tore her apart.

Katie began searching, and as a result of a long journey of spiritual growth and discovery, felt a call to mentor other searching women. To get to that point, Katie had to overcome the noise and confusion in which she found herself. She was trying to numb her emotional pain with travel, shopping, and work. Her purpose during that time was simply numbing her pain. And the anger, hurt, and bitterness she harbored kept her from hearing God's voice for years.

Today, Katie is a licensed minister at Rick Warren's Saddleback Church in California, where she heads up a ministry which trains life purpose coaches. She is also the author of *Pathway to Purpose*, a series for women. She believes we can best find our purpose with a mentor at our side. Mentors or advisors, Katie believes, help us reach the next mile marker and prepare us for the challenges that lie ahead.

Katie says God used her tough experiences to prepare her to minister to others. Through the hope God gave her day by day, she can now offer hope to others.

"In the end," Katie says, "Purposeful living is about hope. If you can hang onto the hope that God does have a plan for your life, as the Bible promises in Jeremiah 29:11,[7] you'll make it through the tough days ..."[8]

Purpose and Health

I remember reading a story years ago about a physician who treated cancer patients. He talked about one of his patients, a landscape architect, who seemed to defy all the odds. Years after other patients with the same type of cancer had died, the landscape architect was as active as the Energizer bunny. Every time the man came in for treatment, reported the doctor, he talked about his purpose. He had to make some new apartment complex, commercial building or park more beautiful. He lived to create beauty and he knew it. The doctor finally concluded the strong sense of purpose was actually keeping him alive because, strictly from a medical standpoint, he should have been long gone.

A recent study reported in the *Health Day Reporter* confirms the doctor's conclusion. Patricia A. Boyle, PhD, and her colleagues from the Rush University Medical Center studied 1,238 older adults who were already participating in ongoing research studies at Rush. The participants, averaging age 78, were all dementia free when the study began. They were asked questions about their purpose in life, rating themselves in different areas meant to measure the tendency to derive meaning from life and to feel progress in achieving goals. The average score was 3.7 out of a possible 5.

When comparing scores (after adjusting for age, sex, education, and race), Dr. Boyle and her assistants found that those with a higher sense of purpose had about half the risk of dying during the five-year follow up period as did those with a lower sense of purpose, even after controlling for such factors as medical conditions and disability. "What this is saying is, if you find purpose in life, if you find your life is meaningful and if you have goal-directed behaviour, you are likely to live longer," she said. Boyle believes the new study is one of the first large-scale investigations to examine the link between life purpose and longevity.[9]

People with a low sense of purpose would answer questions with comments such as "I sometimes feel as if I've done all there is to do in life;" or "I used to set goals for myself but now that seems like a waste of time;" and "My daily activities often seem trivial and unimportant to me."[10]

Finding Purpose Through Pain

Many people actually find their ministry or purpose through their darkest experience. Look at Chuck Colson. A rising political star and close advisor to President Richard Nixon, he went to jail for his participation in the Watergate

24

scandal. After serving his time, he found he could not forget the men still in prison. Having become a Christian in prison, he felt called to establish Prison Fellowship Ministries which now ministers to inmates in many countries around the world.

I have a dear friend, (I'll call him Gary), whose wife was on the ValuJet plane that crashed in the Florida Everglades in 1996. Gary and his wife had been to Miami to attend their daughter's college graduation from the University of Miami. He had to come home immediately for a business meeting but his wife stayed another day or two to help their daughter pack. She had been scheduled to fly back on Delta, but arrived very early at the airport and was told she could get on the ValuJet plane which left almost immediately. When Gary was called on the golf course by his law partner who told him ValuJet was desperately trying to get in touch with him, he said "Why? My wife was flying Delta." But he called, and learned the devastating news – she had transferred to ValuJet at the last minute.

Many people actually find their ministry or purpose through their darkest experience.

Almost immediately, Gary sought ways to comfort the other families who lost loved ones on that flight. He began to learn what he could about airline safety and wound up testifying before Congress. Anytime there was a commercial airplane crash anywhere, he went to see what he could do to be of assistance to the victims' family members. He built an entire ministry in response to his greatest tragedy.

The experiences we learn and the new skills we develop in the midst of our greatest challenges are invaluable and can be tremendously helpful to others who might have to go through something similar. Using our hard-earned knowledge and wisdom to help others brings meaning to life's tragedies. Many scholarships have been established by families who lost college-aged children. Large donations to hospitals and research facilities have been made to treat and cure diseases that claimed the lives of the donor's family members. Purpose, large and small, can be – and often is – forged in pain.

Goals and Purpose

As Christians, our real purpose is to glorify God and lead others to Him, as we discussed in the beginning of the chapter. But how many different ways are there for us to do that? And that's part of the plan. One person may do it on the tennis court, another serving in the armed forces, and another teaching on a college campus. God has His men and women strategically placed to reach as many people as possible for Christ. The real purpose of our lives is actually a by-product of our goals and chosen professions.

Buckminster Fuller, one of the great thinkers of the 20th century, explained this concept in his book, *Synergetics*. He called it precession. Suppose, he said, the honey bee has a life purpose. What would it be? To pollinate plants and keep life on earth going. But to the honey bee, that is not her thought. She gets up each morning to achieve her goal of collecting nectar to make honey. The real purpose (to pollinate plants) is a by-product of the goal. If the goal were our true purpose, said Fuller, once we achieved it, we'd stop. Then, the side effects would stop and our true purpose would be frustrated.[11]

We must, if we can agree with Fuller, set the goal that creates the right side effects and to which we can commit for about 20 years. We should set a goal, he says, that improves the quality of people's lives.

For example, suppose Eleanor sets a goal of becoming a physician so that she can help people heal and maintain health. This will certainly improve their lives. Depending on her chosen specialty, she will have to train from six to ten years after college. Once she is fully trained, as she goes to the hospital every day she will have opportunities, through her skill, training, knowledge, compassion, demeanor, words, and integrity, to glorify God and, on occasion, to tell her patients about Christ, perhaps even leading them in the prayer of salvation. If Eleanor were to say, after she reached her goal of being a fully trained physician, "Well, that's it. I'm done. I've achieved my goal," the side effects (true purpose) would stop.

Well, you say, looking at it that way, God doesn't really care what goal we set. Oh yes He does! Fuller suggests a **God cares about the goals we set.** system called "Listening to the Taps on the Shoulder" to know whether or not we have set the right goals for ourselves.

If we've set a goal and are moving towards that goal, and someone recognizes a quality we have in line with that goal, it's a positive tap. If Bob has set a goal of becoming a veterinarian, and his brother's new girlfriend, not knowing his goal, compliments him on his handling of the family dog and offers to introduce him to her mother, a breeder, a positive tap on the shoulder has occurred. Keep going, Bob. Looks like you've chosen the right career goal for yourself.

Negative taps may come in the form of circumstances appearing to be "bad luck." We should carefully pray through these to see if God is trying to communicate something to us. Be careful of mere negative comments and don't place total reliance on them. Fred Smith, founder of Federal Express, was once told by one of his business professors that the concept of overnight mail to anywhere in the continental U.S. simply wouldn't work. It's a good thing Fred didn't listen to that.

John Wesley, founder of the Methodist Church, used a four-pronged test to determine if a given course of action was God's will:

- Circumstances,
- Whether it is in accord with scripture (or at least not contrary to scripture),
- Whether we have inner peace about it, and
- Whether others who have knowledge and wisdom about the area confirm.

Fuller continues, believing our job is not to make money but to add value to the lives of others. It is unbalanced, he says, to work only for money and only for yourself and your family, but it is also unbalanced to work only for others. How many marriages have fallen apart because of spouses working so hard for others they had no time for their own families?

It is unbalanced to work only for money.

Once we have enough positive taps on the shoulder to confirm we're moving in the right direction, we need to stick with that goal for at least twenty years. It takes that long to make a significant contribution to the area we've chosen. If we are constantly changing direction, we'll never be able to do anything meaningful in any area. By sticking with that area, we have a chance to master it. We can build up a network of contacts, knowledge, expertise, and, as a by-product, wealth.

So, as long as we are moving toward a goal, enjoying what we're doing and adding value to the lives of others by meeting their unmet needs, God will use us to accomplish our true purpose: to glorify God, lead people to Him, and enjoy Him and fellowship with His people forever.

Supercharge Your Career, Mission

If you want to make a *big difference* at whatever you're doing,

28

use leverage. Leverage is doing more with less. I know a man that wrote one article and got it published in nine magazines. That's leverage! Learning to create sixteen outfits with two tops, two pair of slacks and four scarves is leverage. Martin Luther recognized the leverage of prayer. If he had a *very* busy day ahead he spent two hours in prayer instead of his normal one. Reading creates leverage. We can learn a lot by letting others teach us through their books. It can save us huge amounts of time. And, of course, surfing the "Net" provides leverage, as we can almost instantly find answers to many of our questions. Think of ways to use leverage to get where you need to go more quickly and effectively.

If you want to make a big difference at whatever you're doing, use leverage.

Another way to make a big difference is to use synergy. Synergy is when the sum of two or more things together is greater than the sum of the things considered separately. With synergy something "magical" happens. One plus one equals two when the two ones are separate, but put them together and they can equal three, four, five or more.[12]

A good example is the 1980 U.S. Olympic hockey team, a bunch of amateur players molded by their coach into a hockey juggernaut. The coach's first job was to deal with the prima donna mentality of the individual players. In fact, he turned down some incredibly talented skaters just because he didn't think those skaters would ever get it through their heads they had to play as a team, and there was no room for "this is the way I like to play, coach." The team, sooner or later, would have to play the Russians, with players that were at the pro level in the U.S. By skillfully working on his team's collective mentality, the U.S. coach made incredible use of synergy. He crafted a champion team, not a team of champions. The ultimate gold medal won by the U.S. hockey players in the 1980 Olympic Games vindicated the coach's decision to turn down talent if that talent could not be molded.

Abundant living means we live intentionally creating the right side effects to be witnesses wherever we are. God has given each of us different gifts and talents and He will lead us to the area where we should be working.

Chapter 3

AN ABUNDANCE OF MENTORS

Chris Langan piqued the interest of the American people when he appeared on the American television quiz show *1 vs 100*. The show features a superstar "brainiac" who faces off against a crowd of 100 (the "mob"). The brainiac must be smart enough to answer more questions correctly than the entire mob. The top prize is $1,000,000.

The host of the show, in introducing Chris Langan, reported that he had an IQ of 195 (Einstein's was supposedly 150). Well, the brainiac did, in fact, beat the mob, but when his winnings totaled $250,000 he chose to quit while he was ahead, apparently calculating the risk of continuing to win against 100 people.

We might imagine someone as brilliant as Chris Langan would have a Ph.D. in physics from one of our leading technical institutions or maybe be a professor of philosophy at an Ivy League school. In fact, he got a perfect score on his SAT, even after dozing through part of it.[13]

But Chris Langan never finished college. Today, he is working on a theory of the universe in his spare time. He is a farmer – living on a horse farm in Missouri.

Why? Why didn't this great intellect receive a Ph.D. and go on to teach, research, and write, contributing greatly to his chosen field?

Chris Langan is the product of negative mentoring. He was raised in a very poor family with an alcoholic father. The family barely made it, and knowledge of college applications, loan forms, and any sense of entitlement of how to speak up for himself simply did not exist.[14]

He did win a scholarship to Reed College in Oregon, but after a year or so his mother failed to send in the financial aid form, so he lost his scholarship and was not allowed to continue. He went to find out why and the financial aid office just told him they gave his scholarship to someone else. No counseling, no mentoring, nothing. He left before final exams, resulting in a string of Fs on his record.[15]

Positive mentoring can work wonders.

After working for a while, he enrolled at Montana State University. He had car trouble and couldn't get to his scheduled class at 7:30 a.m. He went to his advisor and requested a transfer to the afternoon section of his class. His advisor denied it based on his string of Fs at Reed. Again, no counseling, no mentoring, no concern for Chris as a person. So Chris Langan decided he'd had enough of the system of higher education in America and dropped out permanently.[16]

How sad. No one to mentor and encourage this young man with the great mind. No one to take an interest in him and try to understand and help him. What a waste to our country, and all because no one took the time to care.

On the other side of the coin, let's look at what a little positive mentoring can do for a gifted individual. We'll switch gears from looking at someone talented intellectually to looking at someone talented physically. Anyone who watched the 2008 Summer Olympic Games in Beijing, China could not help but enjoy the nail-biting swim meets featuring Michael Phelps, who went on to win eight gold medals, the most any athlete has ever won in a single Olympic game. As we watched him outmaneuver and outrace one opponent after another, the sports announcers filled us in on how he got to where he is today:

- As a toddler in a stroller, he used to watch his two older sisters practice swimming. One of his sisters tried out for the 1996 Olympic team but didn't make it. But he saw how hard she worked and trained.
- At age 11, he attended the 1996 Olympic Games in Atlanta and watched U.S. swimmers Tom Malchow and Tom Dolan, dreaming he would one day swim on the U.S. team.
- Back home in Baltimore, he was first introduced to his coach, Bob Bowman, at age 11.
- Bowman recognized Phelps's gift and started to really work with him, teaching him technique, discipline, and diligence.
- By age 15 he began watching videos of Ian Thorpe ("Thorpedo") the most prominent swimmer in the 2000 Summer Olympics. (When someone dared compare Phelps to Thorpe, Thorpe's coach said to compare anyone to Thorpe was ridiculous).
- Phelps began reading books about other sports champions, like Lance Armstrong and Vince Lombardi.
- All the while his mother, Debbie, and his coach, Bob Bowman cheered, encouraged, sacrificed, and believed in him.
- So Michael Phelps had many actual and virtual mentors before he became the winningest Olympic champion ever. And because of his gift, coupled with the encouragement of his mentors, we cannot go into a store today without seeing his face on some kind of box.

Why Do We Need Mentors to Live Abundantly?

There are many reasons why mentors matter. Mentors pass on knowledge and experience to the next generation. Henry Alford, author of How to Live: A Search for Wisdom from Old People, says "[H]uman beings are one of the few species that lives long after the age at which we procrete. Why ...? I think it's because old folks serve – or have, until the middle part of the last century or so – as the keepers of wisdom in society; as an old African saying runs, 'The death of an old person is like the burning of a library.'"[17]

Old folks serve as the keepers of wisdom in society.

Mentors, both actual and virtual, serve us in many important ways.

1.) They enhance growth and confidence in us.

When we are young we can't see our strengths and weaknesses (particularly our strengths) nearly as well as the adults in our lives can. If we are fortunate enough to have good, caring adults around us (parents, grandparents, youth directors at church, big brothers or big sisters) they can point us toward our strengths and encourage us to develop them. Often, young people are intimidated by people who are ahead of them in age and skill development, and without the encouragement of mentors they could believe they don't have what it takes to pursue a chosen career or path.

This happened to our daughter. She is (and has always been) very good in math. Today she is a pension actuary (mathematician) for an actuarial firm that does pension consulting. In order to become an actuary, the candidate must pass a series of 11 or 12 exams. When our daughter was just starting down this road, with one or two exams under her belt, she became very discouraged. I vividly remember her telling me one day she just couldn't do it – it was too hard. I looked her straight in the eye and said, "Oh yes you can. You are as good in math as any actuary in this country and don't you let anybody tell you otherwise." I was privileged to be a mentor to her that day, grabbing my daughter from the jaws of discouragement and setting her back on her chosen career path.

My mother, of course, mentored me. I remember wanting to be a cheerleader in high school, but in order to try out in front of the student body all candidates had to pass a tumbling test first. I was not as agile as some of the other girls and came home from school one day very discouraged. I told my mom I didn't know if I would make the varsity cheerleading squad. I wasn't as good as the other girls. Mom, characteristic of her wit and wisdom, said, "I'll tell you one thing. You certainly won't make it if you don't try out." I mulled that one over, figured I had nothing to lose, then tried out and made the squad. I loved every second of that experience, but I would have quit had it not been for my mother's mentoring.

2.) They hold us accountable.

Our church has a mentor program for the youth. Adults sign up to be mentors, go through training, and are assigned – first a grade, and then six or seven students in that grade to mentor. We write notes, attend an event those students participate in monthly, and get to know them at youth gatherings. I signed up but had my doubts at first about how the kids would like it. I have been amazed at how much they seem to appreciate having us "old folks" around!

A couple of weeks ago I wrote a note to one of my students, mentioning I knew his parents and grandparents and was sure, based on those genes, he must be very smart (even though I had no personal knowledge). I was amazed when he came up to me at church, after receiving that note, and asked me if I would hold him accountable to read the Bible through in a year! Wow. What a wise young man. To seek someone to make sure he does what he has proposed to do. We are in the process of working out the details of exactly how that will happen, but I'm sure, if we stick with what we work out, at the end of a year he will have read the Bible through, because I intend to be on the case, to hold him accountable to his own goal.

3.) They teach us to be servant leaders.

Jesus was the ultimate mentor. During His life, He poured Himself into 12 disciples, knowing they would have to carry on His ministry and teach others all that He taught them when He was gone. As a mentor, Jesus served His disciples and taught them how to pray, heal, preach, love, and rely on God the Father as their source.

As the disciples gathered with Jesus for the last supper, Jesus took off His robe, put on an apron, and stooped to wash their feet, drying them with the apron. Peter, incensed that his master should stoop to such a lowly task, protested. Jesus firmly told him that if He didn't wash Peter's feet, Peter couldn't be part of what Jesus was doing.

After completing the foot washing exercise Jesus, noting He was their master and teacher, told His disciples that, even as He washed their feet, they should go out and wash each other's feet. The message was clear – the leader serves.[18]

In fact Jesus, Who was a master and teacher to thousands upon thousands of people, spent His entire ministry serving, with very little if any thought of His own comfort or needs. He went about teaching and healing. He encouraged the oppressed,[19] He defended the accused,[20] and He poured himself into His inner circle of 12.[21]

Even today, Jesus continues to lay down His life for us as He intercedes for us before the throne.[22]

As mentors serve their mentees through spending time with them, sharing in activities together, and encouraging them (laying down their own lives for those they are mentoring), the mentees see what servant leadership is all about.

4.) Mentors provide wise counsel for us.

When St. Francis of Assisi first committed himself to full-time Christian service, he didn't know if he should spend his time closeted in the monastery in prayer or go about preaching the Word. Francis didn't trust his own line of communication to heaven so he called in two of his mentors, Sister Clare and Brother Silvester, and asked them to gather their disciples and pray for direction. Within a few days both came back with the same answer: he should not hide his gift but should go about preaching. St. Francis, delighted to learn his divine assignment, jumped up and said, "Let's go!"[23]

Mentors can be more objective than we ourselves when counsel is needed. And they can point out things to us that we might overlook. How wise of St. Francis to seek counsel from those he knew stayed close to the Father's throne. If we know our mentors are wise and have our best interests at heart, we should indeed give weight to their advice and counsel. And if we know, as St. Francis of Assisi knew, that those mentors are experienced in hearing God's voice, how much more should that weight be given!

Recently I found myself in a jam and consulted two of my prayer warrior mentors for advice. How affirming that they both came back with the same words of encouragement to me. I do not, by any means, believe it was a coincidence.

5.) Mentors show us how to live by being our role models.

One very successful real estate agent said she was often asked by young people entering the profession what they should do. Her answer:

"I am often asked by new real estate agents, 'What's the very first thing I should do when I begin my career?' They are usually shocked by my answer. They expect me to say, 'Learn how to use the MLS' or 'Learn how to prepare a CMA.' Instead, I tell them... 'Have lunch every day of the week with a top agent. The years of knowledge and practical experience you will gain is absolutely invaluable.'" [24]

In other words, watch what the most successful agents do and follow their lead. If they spend most of their day meeting with clients, then you do that. If they make three speeches per month on developments in the real estate field, then do likewise. Copy them, or at least copy their behavior as it relates to selling real estate. They know what works.

Whenever we see someone who is where we would like to be in a certain area, we should consider that person our role model in that area (actual or virtual) and emulate him to the best of our ability. Showing is always better than telling.

6.) Mentors pass on knowledge and experience to us.

Jennifer Thomson, in an article "The Role and Importance of Mentors"[25] says, "Mentors matter! ... Passing on knowledge and experience to the next generation is perhaps one of the fundamental roles, some would say the fundamental role we have to play here on earth."

A couple of years ago I attended my niece's high school graduation. She went to a private school and there were about 95 seniors graduating that year. The headmaster gave short one- to two-minute speeches about all the seniors, highlighting their interests, activities, and where they were going to college. Four or five of the seniors were selected to perform. One of the graduates played a difficult classical piece on the piano and the audience was thrilled. When it came time for the headmaster to tell us about this young man, we learned that both of his parents were piano professors at a local university. All I could think was, "Thank goodness they passed all that knowledge on to their son and made sure he did what he needed to do to continue the family tradition."

Passing on knowledge and experience to the next generation is one of the fundamental roles we have to play.

How do we learn to do worthwhile and significant things? Someone takes the time to teach us. Mentors taught me to:

Ride a bike
Water ski
Do a handspring
Bake bread
Use the Internet
Email
Pray
Sew
Knit
Draft legal documents

Study the Bible
Write a term paper
Counsel battered women
Use software programs
Train my dogs
Manage money
Type
Clean my house
Get old stains out of fabric
Grow spiritually

And *so* much more. Who are your mentors? And what areas of knowledge and expertise are you passing on to others? As we have received, so must we give.

Chapter 4

AN ABUNDANCE OF PROSPERITY

$\mathcal{T}$wenty-five years ago I started my own law firm. I signed a lease for three years and hired a secretary. I was open for business. Stationary and business cards were printed. Every day I would have lunch with a referral source. I accepted every speaking engagement offered. Every morning I parked the car in front of the office and prayed for clients before going inside.

It was slow getting started. I was doing everything I knew to do, but still some weeks it seemed as if nothing was happening. One slow day I was particularly discouraged. I decided to go to the nearby mall and just walk around to get my mind off the business. As I walked I prayed, "God, I'm doing everything I know to do here. No one is calling. If you want me to fail, I'm willing to fail. Just show me."

As I prayed this prayer, I was walking into a bookstore. The store was displaying a book it expected to be a bestseller. There was a table full of these books right up front and several of them were standing upright to show off the title.

Head hanging, I looked up. The book title jumped out at me: *Pray to Win: God Wants You to Succeed.*[26] I was right at the table so it hit me from the right, left, and center. I couldn't believe it. Tears formed quickly as I realized God was responding directly and immediately to what I had just prayed.

With a much improved spirit (and the grateful owner of a new book!) I went back to the office to thank God that it was NOT His plan for me to fail, but to succeed.

The Prosperity Gospel

Despite my personal experience and my belief that God does want us to prosper financially,[27] there are certain requirements that must first be met before this can happen. Even as God wants us to be healthy,[28] if we violate the rules that allow us to be healthy, it's not going to happen. If I put too many powerful "recreational" drugs in my body, I might even wind up dead. If I am a chain smoker, I'm just inviting in a host of physical problems. If I pay no attention to diet, get no exercise, and never go to a doctor or health department for vaccine or checkups, I am not nearly as likely to stay healthy as someone who does.

For us to experience abundance in the area of financial prosperity, we must:

- Be diligent (Prov. 28:19),
- Be honest (Prov. 21:6-7),
- Be generous (Prov. 28:27),
- Honor God with the first of our earnings (Prov. 3:4-10), and
- Be frugal (Prov. 21:17).

Because financial prosperity is only part of total prosperity, we must also keep it in proper perspective (Prov. 10:15, 18:11, 11:4, and 11:28). True prosperity includes joy and peace. There are a lot of rich people who are miserable, restless, and unhappy.

Paul warns us that the love of money is the root of all evil and can present many foolish and hurtful lusts.[29] It's easy for the desire for riches and financial prosperity to become an idol, and so we are warned. We are also told not to store up for ourselves treasures on earth where thieves can steal and where stock market crashes, inflation, unscrupulous financial "advisors," and a host of other unfortunate elements can dissipate wealth.[30] Even if none of these things happen, we know we can't take it with us.

Yet, we need money to pay our bills, send our kids to college, retire, pay taxes, and contribute to God's work here on earth. And we are told that God is able to make *every favor and earthly blessing* come to us in *abundance* so that we may *"always and in all circumstances and whatever the need be self-sufficient, possessing enough to require no aid or support and furnished in abundance for every good work ..."[31]*

The Great Debate

Christian leaders in the United States today do not agree on the so-called prosperity gospel. On September 18, 2006, Time magazine framed the debate with the cover story title: "Does God Want You to Be Rich?" In the article, Time reported, that of the four biggest megachurches in the country, three—Joel Osteen's Lakewood in Houston, T.D. Jakes' The Potter's House in South Dallas, and Creflo Dollar's World Changers near Atlanta – are Prosperity or Prosperity Lite pulpits.

When God gives us a blessing, it is so we can bless others.

Rick Warren, whose church rounds out the "four biggest," is the article's chief critic of the prosperity gospel. Warren says that the idea God wants everybody to be wealthy is "baloney." He says there are many faithful Christians who live in poverty and

43

to believe wealth is for everyone creates a false idol.[32]

What are we to make of all this? We know from the Bible that the power to get wealth is from God.[33] We also know when God gives us a blessing, it is so we can bless others with it.[34] I think we would all agree that while God does want us all to be healthy, He does not want us all to be so blessed physically that we can play professional baseball or basketball. After all, we do need some people out there doing other things. And we know God does not gift everyone mathematically or musically or artistically. People have different gifts and talents so we can get it all done. We need each other and that is part of the plan.

When God does bestow a blessing upon us, there is a responsibility that goes with it. There is also a downside to every gift. For those to whom God gives the power to become wealthy, much is expected. These are the men and women who will be expected to contribute great sums to build hospitals, houses of worship, stadiums, orphanages, museums, parks, and schools and universities. They will be called upon to provide resources for caring for the poor, the hungry, the sick, and the homeless. They will wonder if anyone loves them for themselves, or if it is only because they have money that people are so attentive and accommodating. People with great wealth also have to worry about it – how to invest it, how much to leave to their children, how not to ruin their children with it, how to protect it from those that would sue them, or even worse, how to protect their children from those who would kidnap them for the ransom money.

When God does bestow a blessing there is a responsibility that goes with it.

While great financial wealth is one of God's blessings for those who love Him and are called according to His purpose, it, as all gifts, has a dark side. The challenge is to keep the wealth in perspective and see it as a tool to bless others, not to allow it to become a tyrannical, controlling master.

The bottom line of this great debate for me is this: While God wants us all to have abundant resources to pay our bills, provide for our families, and engage in and contribute to the ministries to which He has called us, He has chosen some (and not all) to bless extraordinarily from a financial standpoint. And those to whom He has given such an ability to get wealth will be held accountable at a high level. In the parable of the talents, the servant who received two talents and returned two, received the same praise from his master as the one who received five and returned five.[35] But the master did expect more from the servant to whom he had given more.

God Provides for Ministry

My husband and I have a small foundation, Encouragement Unlimited, Inc. Once a year we sponsor a seminar for the women in the Atlanta Shelters. We bring them into a lovely retreat center not far from Atlanta and spend at least one full day (sometimes an entire weekend) ministering to them with music, speakers, and fun and games. We always have a great time and always share Jesus with them. Those of us who participate get more out of it than the women who come.

God provided millions of dollars to care for orphans in England.

What amazes me is that, as we approach the seminar date every year, we start getting calls from people and corporations that want to contribute either money or gifts for the women. This year one of my friends living in New York called up a week before the seminar (not even knowing about the seminar) and said she was going to send the foundation a check that wound up covering half the cost of the entire event.

45

Another friend called and said she was donating CDs for the women. Yet another friend had books for them. And a hosiery factory in Kentucky sent a box of two hundred pairs of high quality socks, packaged two to a bag, for us to give to the ladies.

I am so grateful when I see God's provision in such a dramatic way. It makes me realize God always provides abundantly for His work.

One of the great stories of God's abundant provision is the building of the great orphanage covering 13 acres on Ashley Downs in Bristol, England. George Müller, a Prussian who had a less than saintly beginning in life, was led to London after his seminary training to minister to the Jews because of his proficiency in the Hebrew language. There he became very ill and was advised to go to the country for his health. He went to Devonshire and met a Spirit-filled minister who helped him to understand the role of the Holy Spirit in interpreting the Holy Scriptures.

When he returned to London his soul was on fire for God, and he felt compelled to work for the salvation of souls. He married a like-minded woman from Devonshire named Mary Groves and became pastor of Ebenezer Chapel there. As

God always provides abundantly for His work.

pastor, he refused to accept a salary for his work and discontinued the practice of pew rental, a means of church support that he found contrary to Scripture. He and Mary told their needs to no one except the Lord. Sometimes rumors circulated that they were starving, but their income was actually greater than before. After working in Devonshire for a while he was profoundly impressed that the Lord wanted him to work in Bristol. The Providence of God opened the way and it seemed in harmony with the Word of God. So Müller had the "triple braided cord" - the Word, the inner witness, and God's provision, confirming this new direction for his ministry.

Müller began his ministry in Bristol as co-pastor at the Gideon and Bethesda chapels. In a short time the membership there quadrupled. Ten days after the opening of the Bethesda chapel, there was such a crowd inquiring as to salvation, it took four hours to minister to them. After two years Müller started the Scripture Knowledge Institution for Home and Abroad to aid Christian day schools, assist missionaries, and circulate the Scriptures. Through this institution God put it in Müller's heart to build orphanages. He had, at the time, only two shillings (about fifty cents) in his pocket. Without making his needs known to any person but to God alone, over $7 million was sent to him for the building and maintaining of these homes for the orphans. He built five immense buildings of solid granite, able to accommodate up to 2,000 children. Through his fervent prayers alone he received the means to feed them, day by day, for 60 years. In all the time that Müller had charge of the homes, the children did not have to go without a meal. If ever they did, Müller said, he would take it as evidence that the Lord did not want the work to continue. Sometimes mealtime was almost at hand before the food arrived, but never once was it late.

Surely God provided abundantly for this work of His through His servant George Müller.[36]

Tithing, the Key to Financial Prosperity

George and Mary Müller gave away everything they received in excess of what was required to meet their daily needs, and we have just seen how God provided for them. Few of us have risen to their level of faith and probably are not going to, at least not at first. But we can all take up the challenge found in God's Word in Malachi 3:10:

Bring all the tithes, the whole tenth of your income, into the storehouse, that there may be food in My house, and

47

prove me now by it, says the Lord of hosts, if I will not open the windows of heaven for you and pour you out a blessing, that there shall not be room enough to receive it.

Dear friends, this verse is talking about financial abundance. We will have so much we won't have room for it all. I can tell you from personal experience that it is absolutely true, as paradoxical as it may seem.

Years ago, I felt called to go to law school. It was not the best time for my husband and me by any stretch of the imagination. He had just started a law practice with two of his law school classmates. They had no clients. In addition, Emory University, the local law school and a private university, was not cheap. So we had high tuition and no income.

I realized even then (I was in my twenties at the time) we needed a radical financial plan. I also knew that if the vision was truly from God, He would provide. If not, we'd fall flat on our faces. But I had spent time on my knees about this, and my husband agreed, so we took the giant leap of faith.

We had heard of the concept of tithing, which as far as we could tell meant giving 10 percent of all our income to the Lord's work. We'd never tried it, but we decided our radical financial plan would be to give 10 percent of anything we received in any form to our church. That was it. Tithing either worked or it didn't. There was no Plan B. We had to have faith in the biblical principle.

We simply stood on God's Word in Malachi 3:10.

This was quite a switch from our normal mode of giving, which was to put $5 in the offering plate about once a month. We were desperate, however, and desperate times call for desperate measures.

What happened for the next three years (the law school years) was nothing short of a financial miracle. I've often said it would have been worth those three years in law school even if I'd never practiced law a day in my life just to see God working out the miracle for us. All the while my husband was in his brand new law practice with his two buddies, taking whatever work they could get, with no security at all.

The first thing that happened to us was my mother-in-law's review of her financial records. She discovered she had spent more educating her daughter than her son (my husband) and wanted to even the score. So, she sent my husband a check to make everything perfectly equal. Wow! I was impressed. We gave 10 percent to the church and used the rest for law school tuition.

Thereafter, various relatives would send checks to us in the mail, probably because they had heard of our absolutely crazy endeavor and felt sorry for us. Aunt Mary in New York would send checks from time to time – always with a two- to three-page letter which we couldn't read (because her handwriting was illegible). But we could read the check! My precious grandparents, Bobo and Granddaddy, sent checks. Cousin Harriet, on the faculty at Emory, arranged for student loans for me through the loan office. And after I made it through the first year without them, my wonderful, sweet parents sent significant checks to help.

I remember vividly one Friday afternoon sitting in my car outside of the law school. Tuition was due on Monday morning, and we didn't have it. "Lord," I prayed, "I'm putting this problem in Your hands. If You want me to finish, please send the money. If You don't, it's fine with me. But, if You do, I need [I named the amount of tuition]."

As soon as I had finished praying, I remembered we would be tithing on anything we received, and the amount I had asked for wouldn't be enough. But God was ahead of me. On Saturday morning, I went to the mailbox and there was a check for an amount of money that, after tithing, was exactly what we needed for tuition. Were we ever impressed!

In the meantime, back at the struggling new law practice, my husband had a client in the nursery business. Every time he and his wife would come to Atlanta to see their lawyer, they would bring boxes of fresh vegetables – tomatoes, cucumbers, squash, and okra. The first time my husband brought their gifts home, I began spreading the vegetables out in our kitchen. I filled up

The tithe is seed money. my refrigerator and my kitchen table with them. All of my countertops were covered. I looked down at the boxes and there were still more vegetables. I had nowhere to put them. The words of Malachi rang loudly and clearly in my mind: *"Bring all the tithes ... into the storehouse ... and prove me now by it ... see if I will not open the windows of Heaven for you and pour you out a blessing, that there shall not be room enough to receive it."* I sat down and cried, and then I began giving away vegetables to our neighbors.

By the time I had gotten to my third year of law school, I promised God that if He would keep miraculously providing the money for tuition for me to finish and the money for us to live on, I would seize any opportunity I could to tell people to tithe. In fact, I believe God led me into the area of estate and charitable planning so that I could do this professionally, helping people plan to give some of their resources to the wonderful charitable organizations in this country (and worldwide).

My husband and I came to see during those year that tithing was the best investment we could make from every standpoint and we knew we would never, ever stop.

You see, the tithe is seed money. If a farmer and his family ate all of their produce, saving none of the grain to plant the following year, they would soon have no food. The farmer knows the seed must not be eaten but reserved for the future harvest. And so it is with our money. We must plant some of it in the Lord's field. And when we do, He will ensure our abundant harvest because He is a God of integrity who does what He says He will do.

Chapter 5

AN ABUNDANCE OF PROGRESS

I am writing this chapter on the eve of Barack Obama's inauguration as the first African American president in U.S. history. The *Atlanta Journal–Constitution* reports that sermons preached at large African American churches will be collected for the Library of Congress American Folklife Center to be added to its collection of recordings and documents maintained by the library.[37] Future historians will be able to research the reaction of Americans in 2009 to this historic event.

And why is the American Folklife Center collecting sermons about a presidential inauguration? To use one of my favorite law school terms, *res ipsa loquitur* (the thing speaks for itself). We have finally lived up to the vibrant words of Thomas Jefferson in our Declaration of Independence, "All men are created equal," moving from a nation that tolerated the abominable practice of slavery on July 4, 1776 when the Declaration was signed, to a nation that has elected an African American president as its leader in November of 2008.

We celebrate 232 years of progress as a nation. We know

through our history classes how much this progress has cost, but also know it is more than worth the price we have paid. The Civil War was the deadliest war we have ever fought, and leaders such as the Rev. Dr. Martin Luther King, Jr. risked their lives and safety to march and advocate for equal treatment of African Americans years after the slaves were freed. Now African Americans know that they really can grow up to be president of the United States.

And if Barack Obama had not received his party's nomination, Hillary Clinton would have. So, for the first time in our history we had a serious female presidential candidate. I believe it's just a matter of time until we elect our first woman president. And, as if that weren't enough, John McCain was the oldest candidate ever to seek a first term as president, receiving his party's nomination. As a nation, we nominated and seriously considered candidates who previously would have been passed over.

Progress – the Law of the Kingdom

Progress is the law of the Kingdom of God. Second Cor. 3:18, says, *"And all of us, as with unveiled face, [because we] continued to behold [in the Word of God] as in a mirror the glory of the Lord, are constantly being transfigured into His very own image in ever increasing splendor and from one degree of glory to another; [for this comes] from the Lord [Who is] the Spirit."*

Progress is the law of the kingdom of God.

Paul says it is God's will that we move *"from one degree of glory to another."* Even as we celebrate when our children and grandchildren make progress, God celebrates when we make progress, *"being transfigured into His very own image."*

What able-bodied parent or grandparent would not show up at a child's or grandchild's high school graduation? All kinds of recitals and concerts are staged by teachers to display the progress made by the students that year, and we celebrate and rejoice in the educational progress that has been made.

Progress is good, and we need to experience it in our lives to live abundantly. But we need to be moving in the right direction. Consider what some of our great leaders and thinkers have said:

"The great thing in the world is not so much where we stand as in what direction we are moving."
Oliver Wendell Holmes (American Physician, Poet, Writer, Humorist and Harvard Professor, 1809-1894).

"He who moves not forward, goes backward."
Johann Wolfgang von Goethe (German Playwright, Poet and Novelist, 1749-1832).

"We all want progress, but if you're on the wrong road, progress means doing an about turn and walking back to the right road; in that case, the man who turns back soonest is the most progressive."
C.S. Lewis (British Scholar and Novelist, 1898-1963).

"Human progress is neither automatic nor inevitable … Every step toward the goal of justice requires sacrifice, suffering and struggle; the tireless exertions and passionate concern of dedicated individuals."
Martin Luther King, Jr. (American Baptist Minister and Civil Rights Leader, 1929-1968).

"Scientific progress makes moral progress a necessity; for if man's power is increased, the checks that restrain him from abusing it must be strengthened."

Madame de Staël (French woman of letters and political propagandist, 1766-1817).

"The pursuit of peace and progress cannot end in a few years in either victory or defeat. The pursuit of peace and progress, with its trials and errors, its successes and its setbacks, can never be relaxed and never abandoned."
Dag Hammarskjöld (Swedish Statesman and Secretary General of the United Nations, 1905-1961).

"Progress is a nice word. But change is its motivator. And change has its enemies."
Robert F. Kennedy (American Attorney General and Advisor, 1925-1968).

These and many other thinkers and leaders have expressed thoughts on progress. To summarize the ones quoted here, progress means: 1) moving, not maintaining the status quo; 2) moving in the right direction, a positive direction – or if we are not, doing an about-face; 3) stopping those who would use progress in an evil way; 5) sacrificing, if necessary, and changing; 6) realizing not everyone will support progress because some have a vested interest in maintaining the status quo; 7) proceeding anyway without them.

The *Random House Unabridged Dictionary* defines progress as "a movement toward a goal or a higher degree."[38] In other words, to experience progress in our lives we must be moving toward something and we must have a clear vision of what that is. How else will we know progress has been made? We must have goals. If progress is the end result, goals are the means. If we don't have goals, preferably written ones, we're just bouncing around on the sea of life moving wherever the waves take us. Goals are like a motorboat, bucking the current to take us where *we* have *determined* to go.

Goals – The Key to Progress

Motivational speaker Brian Tracy, who has made thousands of speeches all over the world to help people make progress in their chosen professions, says if he had just five minutes to pass on his best advice to us, it would be this:

- Write down goals,
- Make plans to achieve them, and
- Work on those plans every day.[39]

Why are goals so important? Because once we set the goal and announce this to our mind, our mind sets about creating it. Our thoughts are creative. They form and shape our world.[40]

Tracy notes, however, that most people have no idea how to set goals. For example, *I want to be happier* is not a goal because it is not measureable. How do you know when you are happy enough? To be a *bona fide* goal the goal must be:

- Clear and specific,
- Measureable and quantifiable,
- Believable and achievable,
- In harmony with our other goals, and
- Tied to a date by which it is to be achieved.[41]

For example, if I am trying to lose weight, I might say, "I weigh 120 pounds on June 30 of this year." This is a goal (unless it's June 29 and I'm more than five pounds from my goal!) It's clear, measurable, and believable; it won't conflict with other goals; and it has a date by which it will be achieved.

Tracy says all goals should be written using the "3 P" formula: in a positive, personal, and present tense format.[42]

Here are some examples of the right and the wrong ways to do it:

Right: I (personal) weigh (present tense) 120 pounds (a positive statement) on June 30 of this year. (date)
Wrong: I will not be overweight. (negative)
Wrong: I will lose 30 pounds this year. (future tense)
Right: I am cancer free by June 30 of next year.
Wrong: I will not have cancer anymore. (negative)
Right: I earn $100,000 / per year by June 1 of next year.
Wrong: I will not earn $20,000 per year again. (negative)

Vision Motivates

Goals create vision. With vision we have something to progress towards, until we attain the vision. In fact, one quality of great leaders is their vision. George Washington, elected first president of the United States, was not the most brilliant, best educated, or most articulate man of his time. Benjamin Franklin, Thomas Jefferson, Alexander Hamilton, James Madison, and others surpassed him in these areas. But the man who came to be called the Father of His Country had vision, and he knew how to communicate it.

> *Goals create vision. With vision we have something to progress towards.*

His vision included ideas and goals which remained constant throughout the American Revolution. First, he had to win the war for independence against Great Britain no matter how long it took; next, a republican constitutional government had to be established; and finally, he envisioned the nation as contributing to the uplifting and happiness of the whole world in the years and centuries to come. George Washington not only saw the future of the fledgling republic himself, but painted a picture of it so his fellow patriots could see it as well.[43] No wonder he was chosen for the highest office in the land.

What about you? What is your vision for your own life? Choose three believable goals and write them down following the directions given above in this chapter. Put dates by which you will achieve them. Start small so you will get an immediate sense of accomplishment. For example, if you need to lose 100 pounds and it seems impossible, start with something like:

"I eat only fruits, vegetables and protein from Sunday through Saturday of this week."

You are, by making this goal, starting on your long journey by taking a step you can believe in and achieve.

As you successfully achieve your smaller goals, make your goals bigger. Before you know it, you will have achieved more than you can imagine. You will have made progress!

Chapter 6

AN ABUNDANCE OF HEALINGS

$\mathcal{T}$he Hebrew children left Egypt for the Promised Land. Shortly after God delivered them from Pharoah and his army at the Red Sea, they found themselves in a wilderness with no fresh, clean water to drink. The water they did find was undrinkable and bitter. So, they did the logical thing – they complained to their leader.

Fortunately Moses, their leader, was a man of prayer, and he immediately sent an SOS up to heaven. God graciously responded and showed him what to do. There was a tree near the bitter waters, and God told Moses to cast the tree into the waters. As soon as Moses obeyed, the waters became sweet and drinkable.

As God healed the bitter waters He spoke to the Israelites, saying *"I am the Lord Who heals you,"* and promised if they would obey His commandments and keep His statutes, He would protect them from diseases.[44]

Throughout the Old Testament, God revealed different aspects of His character to His children, and this was the occasion for Him to reveal Himself as the Lord Who heals. Although we typically think of healing in the bodily sense, referring to physical healing, it embraces much more than that. When God revealed Himself as Yahweh *Rophe*, the Lord Who heals, He was healing the bitter waters. The verb from which Rophe is derived, though often referring to physical healing, is also used in other ways – for example: God's healing of water, land, nations, and sin.[45]

To live abundantly, we need to tap into this healing power because there will be many occasions during our lifetimes that some illness, relationship, or situation needs to be healed.

Let's look first at the physical and then the mental and emotional aspects of healing.

Step Number One: An Ounce of Prevention ...

If we are fortunate enough to be healthy, the wisest thing we can do is to stay that way. Good health enables us to be more active, and staying well is much easier than getting well after we have become sick. Or, if we have a minor health problem, then we should deal with it before it becomes significant.

Right after the tragic events of September 11, 2001, I attended a meeting at a local church. The guest speaker that night was television star Dixie Carter.

She posed the question of how we should respond to the tragic events we had just witnessed as a nation. On her list of appropriate responses was, "Get in shape, if you aren't already, and stay in shape if you are." She proceeded to share a family recipe for arthritis she had found personally helpful! If we are healthy, Dixie implied, we are not part of the problem. Our health blesses not only us, but all around us.

So, if we're healthy, let's begin by praying and believing for our continued health. I like to make positive affirmations about my health, such as "I am strong; I am healthy. This exercise is helping to keep me that way."

There are also powerful Scriptures we can confess over ourselves:

"But those who wait for the Lord who expect, look for, and hope in Him shall change and renew their strength and power; they shall lift their wings and mount up [close to God] as eagles [mount up to the sun]; they shall run and not be weary, they shall walk and not faint or become tired. "[46]

"He keeps all his bones; not one of them is broken."[47] (With a mother and grandmother who both suffered from broken hips, this is especially relevant for me).

"Beloved, I pray that you may prosper in every way and [that your body] may keep well, even as [I know] your soul keeps well and prospers.."[48]

When we send out God's Word, it does not return void but prospers in the area where it is sent.[49]

If we continuously sow healthy remarks about ourselves and do all we know to do to stay healthy (eat right, exercise, seek good medical advice when needed), we will reap the harvest of continued good health. My husband and I were discussing how to plan for our retirement at the dinner table recently. "Well," I said, "whatever we do, we need to plan to have enough income to live on well into our nineties."

If we continuously sow healthy remarks and do all we know to stay healthy we will reap the harvest of continued good health.

When we make these kinds of positive affirmations, our comments seep down into our subconscious minds and our subconscious minds kick in to bring about the result.

"Life and death are in the power of the tongue,"[50] Proverbs reminds us.

Step number one in any health program is *staying* well. Let's do everything we can to convince ourselves we are going to do just that.

Encountering Illness with Faith

Unfortunately, we may not be able to keep ourselves healthy on a permanent basis: accidents, genetics, contagious diseases, and toxic environments may get the better of us at some point. How do we get healed if the healers (doctors, nurses, pharmacists) can't help us or can do only so much?

The Prayer of Faith

There are many examples of healing in response to faith and believing prayer. Jim Glennon, in his insightful book, *Your Healing is Within You*, recounts the story of little Graeme, who, as he grew from a toddler to a child, developed a pronounced hump in the upper part of his back. A specialist was sought and his parents were told that several of his vertebrae had collapsed, compressing his chest and affecting his heart. The medical experts advised that little could be done for their "hunchback" son.

Graeme's parents realized help would have to come from beyond any human resource. They began reading the Bible and found it promised the prayer of faith would heal the sick.[51] They claimed this promise for their son and believed God for an answer. They were prepared to accept a gradual healing if healing did not come immediately.

At first nothing seemed to happen, yet they were not discouraged but kept on believing. After a while, they thought there was a marginal improvement. After more time, they we sure there was a small change for the better. As one little small advance. At the end of three years, ... was completely straight, his hump gone and his chest ...d heart normal.[52] Their faith increased as they thanked and praised God for each new victory until finally, little by little and step by step, their faith prevailed.

Put Your Mouth Where Your Healing Is

Once we begin the faith journey for healing for ourselves or others, we must discipline ourselves to speak in line with the healing. Faith is an emotion or state of mind and may be induced or created by repeated instructions to the subconscious mind. For faith to work, it is essential for us to encourage positive emotions as the dominating force in our minds and to eliminate negative ones. This is not always easy because we may see the effects of the disease and become discouraged.

We should talk to ourselves (in the car, in the office, in the house, wherever we are) and tell ourselves we can get through the treatment and then our life will return to normal. We should write Scripture verses and positive affirmations on index cards and put them wherever we can see them during the day. We should also put pictures of a healthy "us" around the house. We should express optimism to our family and friends and all of this positive talk should be well emotionalized with belief. If we don't line our thoughts and words up with our prayers, we are double-minded and should not expect to receive.[53]

The corollary is that we want to eliminate all obstacles to receptivity of the cure. We need to stay away from negative friends and family members (if possible). If we can't completely remove these negative people from our lives, then we need to be prepared to counter their remarks with positive ones of our own. And we will have to combat an even greater negative force – the negative thoughts of fear and worry. One of the best ways I have found to do this is simply to say (out loud) when the negative thought comes, "Get out. I am not putting up with this garbage one more second."

Actions Speak Louder than Words

During the days of the prophet Elisha, three kings (of Israel, Judah, and Edom) went to fight their rebellious subjects. To get to where the rebels were, they had to go through a wilderness. In the wilderness they could find no water for their men and animals. The King of Judah called for a prophet and was told that the Word of God was with the prophet Elisha. The kings paid Elisha a visit and asked for his help. Elisha prophesied and said, *"Thus says the Lord: Make this [dry] brook bed full of trenches. For thus says the Lord: You shall not see wind or rain, yet that ravine shall be filled with water, so you, your cattle, and your beasts [of burden] may drink."*[54]

No wind, no sign of rain at all, and yet Elisha tells the kings to dig their ditches. Get ready for what you want. Act as if the water were already here. Prepare right now for it. And so the kings dug their ditches and the very next morning, the water came.[55]

The "act as if" principle is very powerful. A friend of mine was trying very hard (without any success) to get pregnant. Finally, she decorated a room in her house as the nursery and furnished it. Bingo! She hit the magic button. Approximately nine months later, a baby was sleeping there. How many mothers do you know who achieved the same result by adopting their first child because they thought they couldn't have one of their own? They then discovered, shortly thereafter, they were pregnant. By acting as if they were natural mommies, they conceived and became, in fact, natural mommies.

One of my favorite stories along these lines involved a pastor's wife in Houston, Texas, who had been diagnosed with advanced, terminal cancer. She was given six months to live. Did she prepare to die? No, she did exactly the opposite. She began to act like she was the one well person in a sea of cancer patients. She got out of her hospital bed and went up and down the cancer ward in the hospital, praying for all the other cancer patients. Today, fifteen years later, she's still praying.

Visualize the End Result

In any sport, great athletes imagine their shot, pass, jump, swing, or whatever they do, before the actual event. Why do they do this? Because it works. Psychologists are often hired to work with great athletes who are in a slump, leading the athletes through visualization exercises to get them back on track. One famous golf teacher says the mental side of golf represents 90 percent of the game, the physical 8 percent, and the mechanical 2 percent.[56]

Shakti Gawain in her book, *Creative Visualization*, says we can help ourselves and others get well by holding and projecting an image of health and well-being in our minds. She suggests four methods for effective visualization for our health:

1. Mentally visualizing health;
2. Verbally affirming our wholeness;
3. Writing affirmations about our health and wellness;
4. Creating notebooks with pictures of what we are affirming.[57]

If we are sick we can imagine a future event (perhaps a child's or grandchild's graduation or marriage) and see ourselves there, completely well and fully participating in all the festivities. This is a great motivator for us.

Or we can see ourselves, even while sick, performing a valuable service to mankind. This gives us a sense of purpose. It may be just returning to our work. It may be praying for or encouraging others who are sick. Some people who violate all of the health rules live to a ripe old age anyway because they have a strong sense of purpose. Sir Winston Churchill drank, smoked cigars, and was overweight, but because of his strong sense of purpose in guiding his country through the difficult days of World War II, he lived well into his 90s. He didn't have time to be sick!

If All Else Fails ...

I once had a high school math teacher whose favorite saying was, "If all else fails, follow the directions!" She loved to point out the instructions in the text book if someone was stumbling along unable to solve a complex problem.

What if we've tried all of the above to no avail? We are still physically ill. What do the instructions (God's Word) tell us to do?

The great apostle Paul found himself in this situation. He had prayed diligently three times for the *"thorn (a splinter) in the flesh"* to be removed, but God did not see fit to do so. Instead, God gently told Paul His grace was sufficient and in Paul's weakness was his strength because God's strength was most effective in Paul's weakness.[58] *"Lean on me, Paul."*

Why would God not remove this thorn? If we believe God is good all the time, we can only conclude God was accomplishing something great through it, whether Paul saw it or not.

TV and movie star Michael J. Fox was diagnosed with debilitating Parkinson's disease as a young man. There is no known cure and the disease forced Michael into early retirement. In his recent memoir, *Always Looking Up*, he says, "For everything Parkinson's has taken, something with a greater value has been given – sometimes just a marker that points me in a new direction that I might not otherwise have travelled. So sure, it may be one step forward and two steps back, but after a time with this disease, I've learned what is important is making that one step count – always looking up."[59]

Michael reports that through his foundation, over $200,000,000 – that's *two hundred million dollars!* – has been raised and disbursed to find a cure for Parkinson's disease. How many people have prayed to God for a cure for this disease? God is answering their prayer.

Sometimes,, we have to step out in blind faith and trust – trust that God is helping us live abundantly despite the illness and that He is using the illness for good, whether we see it or not, for us as well as perhaps many others.

Healing – Beyond the Physical

We began this section by seeing God heal the bitter waters as He revealed Himself as Yahweh Rophe, the healer. Many times healing is needed that has nothing to do with our bodies. A relationship is broken; our finances are a mess; our soul and spirit are sick; a situation appears hopeless and beyond repair. The same God Who heals our bodies can and will heal anything. And the same techniques – believing; prayer; lining up our thoughts, words, and actions with our prayers for healing; and finally total trust (blind faith) in God's goodness – work to heal in all areas of our lives.

> **The same God Who heals our bodies can and will heal anything.**

In his best selling book, *God's Psychiatry*, Dr. Charles L.

Allen notes that our modern word "psychiatry" comes from two Greek words that mean (1) "soul" or "mind" and (2) "treatment" or "healing" – together "the healing of the mind" – or, as the 23rd Psalm puts it, *"He refreshes and restores my life (my self)."*

Because only God can heal the soul, says Dr. Allen, the first and most important psychiatry must be God's psychiatry, which can be found in the best known passages of the Bible.

He describes how he "prescribed" the 23rd Psalm for troubled souls coming to him for counsel and how he would advise them to take it five times a day, meditating on it slowly each time they "took a dose".[60]

The Psalm brings great assurance to us that Our Shepherd is watching out for us, helping us every day to do far more than just exist. Indeed, He is doing all He can to ensure that His sheep live a healthy and abundant life.

Chapter 7

AN ABUNDANCE OF DELIVERANCES

Since 1634, in the village of Oberammergau in Bavaria, Germany, a passion play is performed every 10 years involving virtually the entire population of the town. Tourists come from all over the world to see this historic production. Why? Is it because the people in the village are naturally talented as actors? Or because the set is breathtaking beyond description? While the actors and set may be exceptional, the reason this play attracts the world's attention is because of the story behind it.

In the late fall of 1632 the bubonic plague, known as the Black Death, was sweeping Europe. Antibiotics had not been discovered, of course, and without treatment the bacterial plague killed 50 percent of its victims in three to seven days.[61] The death rate among adults in Oberammergau soared from October of 1632 to March of 1633. The villagers prayed and made a promise to God: If He would deliver them from the ravages of this disease, they would perform a passion play every 10 years. In an apparent answer to their prayer, the adult death rate subsided to one in the month of July 1633.[62] The villagers kept their promise by staging the first production in 1634 and continuing every 10 years to this very day. (The play, lasting seven hours with a meal served during the performance, is now performed in years ending in "0"). Now, almost 400 years later, the descendants of those villagers are still fulfilling their ancestors' promise in gratitude to God for His deliverance from a disaster that only He could have stopped.

God has always been in the business of deliverance. When there is no answer, God is the answer. When I am in a jam, I often remind myself of all the times God delivered the Israelites from their enemies. I am amazed that He never seemed to do it the same way twice. He **When there is no answer God is the answer.** sometimes caused enemy armies to see and hear things that were just not there, resulting in very bad decisions.[63] In one case, the enemies just killed each other off.[64] He has ways too numerous to count to save us from death, disease, enemies, poverty, abandonment, and every other known and unknown form of disaster.

But no deliverance compares with the deliverance from eternal separation from God, that Jesus, the Christ, died for us to enjoy.

Deliverance from Eternal Death

God is perfect. His eyes are too pure to look on evil. He cannot tolerate wrong.[65] Because none of us is perfect, we have a problem. God requires perfection and we simply aren't perfect. There is nothing we can do about it, but God in His great mercy has figured out a way.

Several years ago I was teaching a Sunday School class at our church. The materials gave an illustration of a tough judge known as the "hanging judge" because he always doled out the maximum sentence the law allowed to anyone brought before him. One day a young man accused of DUI came before

70

the judge. As he was brought in, gasps were heard around the courtroom. The courtroom regulars recognized the young man as the judge's own son. What would the judge do, they wondered. Would he be as tough on his son as he was on everyone else, or would he show leniency because he loved the boy so much?

True to his nature, the judge meted out the maximum sentence – $5,000. But then he did a very strange thing. He stood up, took off his judge's robe, went around and stood beside his son, and took out his checkbook and wrote out a check for $5,000 because he knew there was no way his son could pay the fine. With this one act, the judge satisfied the requirements of the law and his love for his son.

The materials went on to remind us that that's what God did when He sent Jesus. Jesus' death on the cross was the "check" God wrote. The "fine" here was much greater than *any* amount of money. It was the life and blood of God's only Son. By accepting Jesus as our Lord, we receive His perfection which is attributed to us. God then sees us, not as we are, but through the lens of His Son's blood, which cleans us up, covers us up, and airbrushes us to perfection. With that, we are able to live in His Presence eternally.

If you have never asked Jesus to come into your life to be your Lord and Savior, exchanging your imperfections for His perfection, I invite you to pray this prayer right now, so that you will not have to live one more minute without the assurance of deliverance from eternal separation from God and the peace of mind that you will be in heaven forever when you die:

> Dear Jesus, I admit I need You. Please forgive my unbelief and the things I have done wrong. I believe You are God's Son and that you paid for all my sins with Your blood on the cross. I call on You to be my Lord and to save me, and I receive Your perfection and Your gift of eternal life. I know I will be with You in heaven when I die. Thank You for saving me. Amen.

Deliverance from Enemies

We all have enemies – people who do not want us to succeed, people who take advantage of us, people who threaten us, people on the other side of issues we feel strongly about, people who betray us in some way. Sometimes these are minor problems and sometimes they are major.

In my law practice over the years, I've encountered my fair share of them. I've been accused of treason, received a death threat, taken clients through many audits with the IRS, and been threatened with lawsuits. None of this is pleasant and sometimes it's downright frightening. But what always helped me get through these trials was the sure knowledge that God does what He says He will do, and the remembrance of the *many* times He delivered His children, the heroes and heroines of the Bible, from their enemies.

When Daniel was thrown in the lions den, the lions could not open their mouths to harm him; when Shadrach, Meshach, and Abednego refused to worship idols and were thrown into the fiery furnace, they were not harmed;[66] when Esther and her people were threatened by an evil prince, God gave her such great favor with the King that he granted her wish to save her people;[67] when Jehoshaphat, King of Judah, who had no army, was attacked by three enemy armies, God caused them to be so confused that they killed each other off.[68]

Perhaps no one had to be delivered from his enemies more often than King David of Israel. Before he became king, even Saul, the reigning king, became David's enemy. In Psalm 18, David calls the Lord his *"Rock," "Fortress," "Deliverer," "keen and firm Strength," "Shield,"* and *"High Tower"* (v.2). He testifies that he will call upon the Lord, who will save him from his enemies (v.3). David confesses to being *"terrified"* (v.4) as death surrounded him.

But David, the great warrior/poet, recounts that in the midst of the terror, God *"drew me out of many waters"* (v.16) and *"delivered me from my strong enemy"* (v.17). Not only did God deliver David, He caused his *"lamp to be lighted and to shine,"* (v.28) which enabled him to *"run through a troop"* (v.29), guided him with *"strength"* (v.32), and made his *"feet like hinds' feet,"* setting him securely in his high places (v.33). God did far more than provide the deliverance David asked for. He used the trials to make David stronger and more capable as a great leader.

As Sarah Young says in her devotional book, *Jesus Calling*, "Abundant life is not necessarily health and wealth, but living in complete dependence on [God]."[69] That's exactly what David was doing.

My friend Barbara ministers to the U.S. troops going to Iraq and Afghanistan out of the Atlanta airport. She gives them camouflage motif scarves printed with Psalm 91. The United States has enemies in those countries and the

Abundant life is living in complete dependence on God.

promises of God's protection for His children in the 91st Psalm are bound to be of great comfort to these young men and women.

I particularly love God speaking in the last three verses of that great Psalm:

"Because he has set his love upon Me, therefore will I deliver him; I will set him on high, because he knows and understands My name (has a personal knowledge of My mercy, love, and kindness –trusts and relies on Me, knowing I will never forsake him, no , never).
"He shall call upon Me, and I will answer him; I will be with him in trouble, I will deliver him and honor him.

"With long life will I satisfy him and show him My salvation."

Deliverance from Physical Danger and Death

Craig Barnes, Pastor of the National Presbyterian Church, in Washington, D.C. (a town that thrives on crisis), had a less than perfect childhood. When he was 16, his mom left his dad, a pastor, and Craig's father lost the church he was serving. Then his dad took off, unable to cope with the failure of his own home. Craig and his older brother, who had dropped out of school to help Craig finish, lived in New York. They decided to hitchhike to Dallas to visit their mom for Christmas. They were on Highway 81 by the Shenandoah Valley in Virginia when a huge blizzard hit. The police closed the highway and there they were – stranded as darkness set in.

To keep themselves warm and together they got competitive. After going through all the sports stats they could think of, they started in on Bible verses. Their dad had made them memorize Scripture as children, so one would call out a verse and the other would have to recite it. Craig's brother pointed at him and said, "Isaiah 43:1-4." Craig responded, "Fear not, for I have redeemed you; I have summoned you by name; you are mine. When you pass through the waters, I will be with you; and when you pass through the rivers, they will not sweep over you ... since you are precious and honored in my sight, and because I love you." Craig says that passage, previously just words, was suddenly full of meaning for him and he knew everything was going to be okay. Not long thereafter a state trooper picked them up and took them to an all-night diner where they spent the night. The next day a trucker took them to Dallas.[70] By remembering God's promise, Craig and his brother found deliverance.

74

I have a highway story of deliverance myself. It was a hot August day and I had travelled from Atlanta up I-85 to a small town in North Georgia to meet with a client. As I do every morning, I had prayed the blood of Jesus over myself and every member of my family before leaving. After the meeting, we went to lunch at a Chinese restaurant with a buffet line. My husband does not like oriental food, so when I get a chance to eat Chinese, I usually eat too much, which is what I did that day.

On the way home, with the hot August sun beaming through the window, and too much food in my stomach, I felt myself getting drowsy. I turned up the air conditioner and slapped my face a few times. Suddenly, I felt the car jolting underneath me. I looked up and realized I was in the median, bouncing on the grass. Then, the car jumped back on I-85. I knew I had gone to sleep at the wheel. I prayed an SOS prayer, "Jesus, help me!"

The car started spinning around. I remember thinking, "This is not safe. I'm spinning around in the middle of I-85. A truck could hit me."

The car started veering toward the right into some trees. I turned the wheel and got it back on the pavement. When it finally stopped I was facing the ongoing traffic, only the "ongoing traffic" was stopped, watching the show. I turned the car around and pulled over to the side of the road. People came running up to me, yelling "Are you all right?"

Yes, there was not even so much as a scratch on my car. I had been delivered from death by calling the name of Jesus, Who literally saved my life that day.

Did I remember to quote Scripture? No – no time for that. I only remembered a name – the Savior's name – and that's all I needed.

Deliverance from Lack

Sometimes I smile at the ways God delivers us from lack and provides for our basic needs – food, clothing, and shelter. He seems to take great delight in doing far more than we could ever ask or think and doing it in ways that make us know it could only be from Him.

Who else could provide manna every morning for the Israelites on their way to the Promised Land?[71] Or provide a coin from a fish's mouth to pay taxes?[72] Or feed a crowd of 5,000 with five loaves and two fishes?[73]

The God who provided thousands of years ago is still doing it today. Clark Cothern is the pastor of the Trinity Baptist Church in Adrian, Michigan. When he and his wife were church planting, their third child was on the way and due in two weeks and the bills were piling up. Nonetheless they gave God a tenth of their meager income, wondering what their baby would wear to the newly planted church's grand opening service. They had given all their baby clothes to an expectant mother in their former church.

The very next day a UPS truck pulled up in front of their house and dropped off a huge box. The return address was in South Carolina but they didn't know anyone in South Carolina.

As they tore open the box, they found several beautifully wrapped packages with a note taped to some photographs: "We asked your mission board for a missionary family to help and they gave us your name and address. Here are the pictures of the baby shower we held for you. We hope you have as much fun opening them as we had wrapping them." Six smiling strangers had signed the card.

That box provided clothes and other items for the new baby. But that was only the beginning. Throughout the year, the UPS driver delivered box after box of unexpected gifts for the baby and for the family's birthdays and Christmas.

One day, the UPS man asked, "Where does all this stuff come from?"

Pastor Cothern replied, "Do you believe God provides?"

In an article he later wrote about this experience, he goes on to tell of the many miraculous stories he and his family witnessed firsthand as sacks of groceries would mysteriously appear in the back seat of their car when funds were low, and help with hospital bills was provided by the church when their daughter broke her arm. He calls these "markers on the ministry highway" and says they are reminders that God never leaves us stranded.[74]

As tangible evidence that we trust God to deliver us from poverty and lack and provide for our needs, we need to take a step in faith and give God one tenth of our income (the tithe). Paradoxically, the way to receive and be delivered from lack is to give.

Paradoxically, the way to receive and be delivered from lack is to give.

The act of giving is our tangible expression of our faith in God to provide. Clark and Joy Cothern gave a tenth of their "meager" income, wondering how they would buy clothes for their baby. God had already moved women they didn't even know to hold a baby shower for them, not once but several times over the course of the year their baby was born.

Yes, we must look to God to deliver us from lack. He alone can provide in miraculous ways.

Deliverance from Self

Finally, God delivers us from the stupid, negligent, careless, and thoughtless things we do ourselves. Let's face it – sometimes our worst enemy is us!

In my weekly prayer group, we have prayed for over a

year for the son of one of our members, a doctor who got in trouble by prescribing drugs over the Internet in order to pick up some extra cash at a time he desperately needed it. The federal government was after him on criminal charges. We prayed over a year that he would not go to jail and that he would not lose his license to practice medicine.

He was scheduled, along with several other defendants, to be tried and was told the trial could last up to three months. One week before the trial was scheduled to begin, his mother called me, praising God with every other word, and told me he had been offered a plea bargain. He would not go to jail and he would keep his license to practice medicine. The only thing he would forfeit would be the job he currently held at the hospital. Wow! I have never heard of such a favorable plea bargain in my life. (Normally, a plea bargain involves going to jail for a lesser period of time than might occur with a jury trial.)

This doctor believed in God and knew we were praying for his deliverance for over a year. He was certainly his own worst enemy, but there is no doubt God was the One who bailed him out.

To live abundantly, we all need to be delivered – not once – but many times during the course of our lives. No two of us are alike, and we will need to be delivered from many different attacks and situations.

Let us stand on and confess the Word of God. Let us call on the name of the Lord Jesus, our High Tower. And let us remember the many times before in our past and in the history of God's children that He has delivered us from every conceivable danger.

"Through many dangers, trials and snares we have already come. 'Twas grace That got us safe thus far, and grace will lead us home."[75]

Chapter 8

AN ABUNDANT INHERITANCE

Sergey Sudev is a journalism student in Komrat, Moldova, a country in Eastern Europe. One day he heard someone knocking at his door. People he had never seen before delivered incredible news: "Your uncle has died. His will left you 950 million euros (about $1,330,000,000)." Sudev was shocked. "Is this a joke?" he asked. He had not seen his uncle for ten years, but after their last meeting, the uncle promptly changed his will to leave his fortune to Sergey.[76]

By any earthly standard, Sergey Sudev received an abundant inheritance. He instantly became one of the richest men in Moldova with no effort on his part whatsoever. The proverbial rich uncle died, in fact, exist for Sergey.

The Inheritance of Legacies

Very few of us, however, have a relative who leaves us with hundreds of millions of dollars. And yet, all American citizens have already inherited a fortune we rarely even think about. Just because we were born in America, we inherit the wealth and legacies of the industrialists and philanthropists that lived and made their fortunes here. Andrew Carnegie used his wealth to build libraries so all citizens would have free access to the great literature of the world. Others, such as J. Paul Getty, built museums to house art treasures, enabling any person who shows up at the door to enter and feast on the masterpieces within. At least for the Getty Museum in Los Angeles, California, admission is free.

Others built hospitals, schools, universities, theaters, roads, bridges, buildings, and all manners of others structures to make our lives easier and better. What did any of us do to aid in building these facilities that were here when we arrived on the planet? In case we're inclined to take this for granted, we need only to look to other areas of the world where no such inheritance exists. In the *New York Times* bestseller *Three Cups of Tea*, we can read the heartwarming story of how Greg Mortenson, an American nursed back to health by the residents of a remote village in Pakistan after a mountain climbing accident, expressed his appreciation by building a school for the children there, who had none. Realizing the great need, he went about raising money and then repeated the process many times over for a part of the world that was very poor. The story of how appreciative the Pakistanis were to have a place to educate their children, thereby guaranteeing them a better life, illustrates how much we in America have – and how much we take for granted.

Our lives are better because of all who contributed through their genius, inspiration and dedication.

And what about the amazing engineering feats, innovative life-changing discoveries, advances in health science, and inspirational books, speeches, and films we have inherited in the realm of intellectual property? Our lives are better because of all who contributed through their genius, inspiration, and dedication.

The progress our scientists have made in eradicating disease is mind boggling. An immunologist who works at

Houston Children's Hospital in Houston, Texas told me that AIDS, for example, which used to be fatal, currently was being treated as a chronic disease and that leukemia, in most cases, could now be cured.

As a child I remember the crippling threat of polio. The very mention of it put fear into the hearts of parents and children who were old enough to understand. The highly infectious polio virus could put its victims in an iron lung for life if, in fact, the victim even survived. When Dr. Jonas Salk discovered the vaccine to prevent it, he was rightly hailed as a national hero. Discoveries in the areas of disease prevention, better nutrition, more accurate diagnoses, and less invasive surgical techniques have extended the life expectancy of the average American from about 48 years one hundred years ago[77] to 78.1 years for babies born in 2006.[78] We inherited all this wealth (for most of us anyway) with no effort on our part.

The Inheritance of Nature

In addition to the legacy left us by the wealthy philanthropists and the brilliant inventors, scientists, engineers, artists, and thinkers in every discipline, we have inherited the spectacular world of nature. How many breathtaking western skies have overwhelmed us as we marveled at the streaks of orange, pink, and golden red splashed across a cornflower blue canvas, celebrating the end of a glorious day and bidding the sun goodnight?

And are we not awed by the majestic live oak trees on our southeastern coast, laden with Spanish moss draped as if it had been carefully placed for a festive occasion? Looking across the rounded tops of the Appalachian Mountains in the eastern United States or marveling at the rugged Rockies in the West, or gazing in wonder at the rim of the Grand Canyon, watching the colors change as the day progresses, is an inheritance without price. We need no money to enjoy any of this.

The Inheritance of Christ

But as fabulous as all of this is, nothing compares to our inheritance in Christ Jesus. Jesus came that we might have life and have it in all of its abundance.[79] As God's heir, Jesus has access to unlimited blessings, eternal life, and heaven itself. Through entering into a relationship with Him, we become the adopted sons and daughters of God, sharing in God's kingdom with Him.

God blesses us with this inheritance when we take the step of asking Jesus into our hearts and lives. Nothing else is necessary, and once we do, we are God's children, equally loved, valued, and treasured. In Christ there is neither Jew nor Greek, slave nor free, male nor female. We are all one in Christ Jesus.[80]

Being one in Christ Jesus is certainly good news because women, African Americans, and others have not always been treated equally, to say the least. Under the Old Testament Jewish law, only sons could inherit from their fathers, and the firstborn inherited a double portion (twice as much as the other sons). A daughter could inherit only if there were no sons.[81] Women had to come under protection of a husband or brother if their father died. Obviously this system had problems, and laws were eventually changed so that women could inherit right alongside their brothers. Thank goodness those old days are gone.

Being one in Christ Jesus is certainly good news because women, African Americans and others have not always been treated equally.

Years ago I was working at a firm as a young attorney. After I'd been working there for a while it became clear to me I was treated differently from the professional men. Partners' comments to me indicated I did not need as much salary, for example. Without bothering to ask or find out any of the details of my home life, they were presuming my husband took care of everything. For all they knew, I could have been a battered wife with a perpetually drunk husband. (Let me hasten to add I was not, am not, and never have been. I have a wonderful husband whom I truly love, but the point is *they didn't know this*.) This hurt me because I knew some of them to be Christians who should have known better.

I sensed, as I never had before, a darkness in this treatment that I perceived as evil. I had never really believed women were discriminated against, thinking it was all in their minds. But when I encountered it up close and personal, all of that changed. I began to cry out to God, asking Him why. I even wondered if God Himself discriminated. God quickly began to show me in a number of ways He did not.

First He reminded me of the Scripture which says *"There is now no distinction neither Jew nor Greek, there is neither slave nor free, there is not male and female; for you are all one in Christ Jesus." (Galatians 3:28).*

Then He brought to my mind His very character, which is now my plumb line for resolving any question I have about God. I knew a God of justice would never discriminate, and the sure knowledge of His

We all inherit equally from God.

character gave me peace. Jesus, who told us if we had seen Him we had seen the Father,[82] treated women as equals at a time in history when that was unheard of. He showed Himself first to His women friends after His resurrection, favoring them with the first sight of the glorious fact.[83]

Finally, He supernaturally brought a wonderful woman minister into my life who shared with me several resources she had uncovered in struggling with her own call into ministry, faced with Paul's teaching that a woman should not teach a man but remain quiet in the church.[84] The bottom line of her research led to the conclusion that Paul was writing at a time when women had no formal education and no experience in going to church, much less teaching anyone. What he said applied to his time, not ours. She felt the call of God to preach and minister, and God gave her the assurance that His daughters today can be as qualified, prepared, and anointed as His sons.

Isn't it wonderful to know our God loves and blesses all children without regard to race, color, gender, or any other external characteristics? We all inherit equally from Him. During my period of grief and despair, I promised God that if He would help me to become a successful and nationally recognized expert in my field, notwithstanding the discrimination I faced, I would write a book telling everyone who would read it that God did not discriminate.

God did far more than I could have asked or thought. He has always helped me succeed with my cases. Every time I needed help, I prayed and He showed me what to do. To the outside world it looked as if I was a great attorney, but I want my readers to know that it was God. So now I'm fulfilling my part of the bargain. This is that book.

So we already have an abundant earthly inheritance. But what is our spiritual inheritance? It's better than anything we can imagine. In broad terms we inherit the Kingdom of God. That includes heaven, salvation, and eternal life (Mark 10:17 and 27 and 1 Peter 1:4); the promises of God (2 Peter 1:4 and Hebrews 6:12); blessings (2 Peter 3:9); and the Holy Spirit, Who is a down payment on all that is to come (2 Corinthian 1:22).

In effect, some of what we inherit spiritually we already have, such as the promises of God, and God within us, the Holy Spirit.

In effect, some of what we inherit spiritually we already have, such as the promises of God and God within us, Who is the Holy Spirit. This is wonderful in and of itself. Have you ever claimed a promise in God's Word? Some promises have conditions attached to them which must be met first, but once we meet those, we can stand on the Word, knowing our God is a God of integrity, and He does not lie.

For example, Proverbs 3:6 says, *"In all your ways know, recognize, and acknowledge Him, and He will direct and make straight and plain your paths."* Here we find a promise of guidance if we acknowledge God as our source. Psalms 91:9-10 states, *"Because you have made the Lord your refuge, and the Most High your dwelling place, there shall no evil befall you...."* We have God's protection if we dwell in Him. These precious Bible promises are part of the "now" part of our inheritance in Christ Jesus.

And the Holy Spirit, God in us, is part of the "now" of our inheritance. Jesus told us it was to our advantage for Him to leave because the Holy Spirit would be sent to live with us and guide us.[85] I have found He guides me even when I don't realize I'm being guided. About five years ago, my elderly dad was not feeling well at all. It was early April and I had been over to see him at his home Saturday morning. I talked to him and my mom and made sure they

The best part of our inheritance is yet to come.

were comfortable, and then I left. That same afternoon, I had a strange urge to go back and see him again, which I did. I sat by his bed, placed ice chips on his tongue, and told him how much I loved him. I assured him, when he asked, that his income tax return would be extended and would not have to be filed on April 15. It was a very special time with him. Unknown to me at the time of that urge, that would be the last time I would see him alive. He died early the next morning. Through the silent guidance of the Holy Spirit, I was able to comfort myself and give comfort to my dad in his final hours on earth.

The "now" part of our inheritance for God's children is wonderful, but the best is yet to come. Even the wealthiest person on this earth will leave all the wealth here when he dies.

Our inheritance includes the new bodies we receive when we die. It's like getting a permanent tooth because we have outgrown the baby tooth. St. Augustine says our new spiritual bodies will be completely restored, immortal, and incorruptible, and not a hair on our heads will perish. Those who die as children will grow up in heaven to be perfect adults. Our bodies in heaven will also be far superior to those we have now. For example, our eyes will be able to see spiritual bodies which our earthly ones cannot now see.[86] It will be a place of 'everlasting felicity' where we will find only honor, peace, virtue, light, health, happiness, freedom, nourishment, plenty, glory, contentment, rest, restoration, and grace.[87] Max Lucado reminds us that in heaven we will be like Jesus. We will have a heart like His: guiltless, fearless, thrilled, worshiping, joyous, and discerning. And, he reminds us, everyone else will be like Jesus as well. No arguments, no jealousy, no insecurity.[88]

Picture the scene – arriving at the pearly gates and seeing streets of gold[89] branching off in every direction, being greeted by Saint Peter, who calls the person who was closest to you on earth (now in heaven) to show you around, and finally arriving at your permanent mansion/home.[90] It is more beautiful, functional, and comfortable than anything that you've ever seen or read about. No expense was spared, no corners cut, no detail overlooked. You can't imagine what a home like this would cost to build, but you don't have to worry about it. You realize your Father is wealthy beyond comprehension and it is His joy and delight to share that wealth with you, His child.[91] Can you even imagine it?

As Christians we are inheriting far more than Sergey Sudev did. In fact, his inheritance is limited and temporary. Ours is unlimited and permanent. We need but to open our eyes to the "now" part of our inheritance and rejoice that the future part is secure in a place where no moth or rust destroys and thieves do not break through and steal.[92]

CHARACTER TRAITS FOR ABUNDANT LIVING

Chapter 9

AN ABUNDANCE OF THE AWARENESS OF GOD'S PRESENCE

God tells us in His Word He never leaves us, so He is always present with us.[93] But to be aware of His Presence brings great joy and power into our lives. The Bible tells us, *"You have made known to me the path of life; you will fill me with joy in your presence, with eternal pleasures at your right hand. ..."*[94] Living abundantly includes living with joy and power over our circumstances.

Twice in my life I have had an overwhelming sense of God's Presence. Both times, I had just laid something on the altar that I had been holding onto for selfish reasons. But when I said, "No more, God. This is not right. I am giving it up." The sense I had of God being with me was so overwhelming that nothing else mattered to me. I didn't care if I lived or died. To die and be forever with God, released from this earthly realm, seemed like a most delightful option. All earthly pursuits of status, recognition, and material things melted away and I saw them for what they were – distractions or hindrances to enjoying the one and only thing that could bring true joy – being with and aware of God in a close, intimate, personal relationship. I was so ecstatic I would not have cared if I had had the lowliest job on the planet or been exiled to Siberia. This powerful awareness, which lasted two or three days, trumped everything.

Although I have experienced an overwhelming sense of God's Presence only twice, I have, on many occasions, sensed God with me. It always brings great peace and a feeling of well-being. God has a habit, I think, of making us especially aware of His Presence when we are experiencing difficulties or hardships.

During the years I practiced law, I worked with special families who had been through extended and painful illnesses with family members before their loved ones finally died. It usually involved one family member – the spouse, typically – living at the hospital with the patient for several months, watching the deterioration and hearing the negative medical reports. Some of these clients were also friends, and when it was over I would ask, "How did you do it? Where did you get the strength to keep going?" One friend said, "It was the awareness of God's Presence that got us through. Without that we would not have made it."

God has a habit of making us especially aware of His Presence when we are experiencing difficulties or hardships.

Another friend told me his wife, the patient, actually saw Jesus standing there in the hospital room with her toward the end of her life. She told her husband to get Him a chair so He wouldn't have to stand up. Although my friend did not see Jesus as his wife did, he felt the Presence nonetheless.

The Presence Overrides Torture

One of the most memorable books I have ever read is *Tortured for Christ*,[95] the story of Richard Wurmbrand and his wife, Sabina. They were tortured for their faith and obedience to God during the communist rule in Romania. Had a movie been made of what was done to them, it would have been R-rated. Don't let the kids see this one. They were tortured physically and psychologically day after day. By any standard it was a grueling experience.

The torture, however, was not what stuck with me. When they were finally released, they found their way to Southern California, where they lived in a delightful climate with abundant freedom, friends, and finances. Richard ostensibly now had the abundant life, as we Americans would describe it. But look at what he wrote about the life he left:

"I can never describe the beauty of [the underground Church]. Often, after a secret service, Christians were caught and sent to prison. There, Christians wear chains with the gladness with which a bride wears a precious jewel received from her beloved. The waters in prison are still. They receive His kiss and His embraces, and would not change places with kings. I have found truly joyful Christians only in the Bible, in the Underground Church, and in prison."

Richard Wurmbrand was saying God's overwhelming Presence was worth more than the treasures of entire kingdoms.

"God Sightings"

Three years ago I went with a group from our church to the Gulf Coast to help the Hurricane Katrina victims. We worked with CityTeam, a ministry that had set up camp for those who came to serve.

We would gather each morning for devotionals before going out to work where we had been assigned. At devotionals we would share "God sightings," evidence of God's Presence there among us. One widow victim told a group member she had prayed for help in getting back into her house. The construction team, she said, was an answer to prayer.

Another shared a story of a woman with two disabled relatives (as well as several able relatives) living in her house, which was heavily damaged by the storm. She had no money to pay for repairs but several groups came to get the framework and walls back in place. Other groups came to paint. The one thing she needed after this was an electrician to get her power restored. One of the painters that came, not knowing he would be needed to do anything but paint, had worked for an electrician for a while but was not licensed. As he saw her need, he volunteered to do the work. God sent him to "paint" just the right house in answer to her prayers.

Some of us were riding along the coast one day, surveying the damage – home after home leveled; debris (one year after the storm) still visible; wrecked cars on top of piled branches. We were feeling a bit depressed when suddenly we came across a sign:

"The Lord is my Rock, my Fortress, and my Deliverer; my God, my keen and firm Strength in Whom I will trust and take refuge, my Shield, and the Horn of my salvation, my High Tower. ... He reached from on high, He took me; He drew me out of many waters ... "[96]

A witness of God's deliverance amidst the deluge!

As we shared our "God sightings" each morning, we were encouraged and strengthened. To know we were the answer to someone's prayer and to see God's provision thrilled us. To see a testimony in the midst of devastation strengthened our faith. Yes, these "sightings" of God, proving His Presence, brought us much joy.

Why the Plum Tree Had Plums

An article in *Leadership Journal* provided evidence that even plants prosper in God's Presence. A church had hired a landscaping company which planted some plum trees in the churchyard. The company told the church, however, that these plum trees would not produce fruit. They were for decorative purposes only. When the trees began to produce, not a few but an abundance of plums, the pastor explained the phenomenon:

> The plum trees experienced the laughter and happy spirit of the children [who play in the churchyard]... They have heard a bell choir from Haiti. They have witnessed a communion service on the front lawn of the church along with evening vespers. Senior citizens who meet in the fellowship hall every Tuesday walk by the trees.
>
> Many families pass by as they come to worship; and the trees watch the joy that comes as these folks leave to face another week after spending an hour in the worship of God. They have heard the singing of hundreds of hymns from the open windows of the sanctuary ...
>
> They have watched the Christmas story recreated each year on Christmas Eve, right under their branches... and, of course, a street full of people who sing carols.
>
> Any tree that has been a part of all of this could not help but respond with a whole chorus of plums.[97]

The trees were in the Presence of God. Jesus said, "I am the Vine; you are the branches. Whoever lives in Me and I in him bears much (abundant) fruit. However, apart from Me [cut off from vital union with Me] you can do nothing."[98] The plum trees knew that.

Brother Lawrence

Brother Lawrence of Lorraine, France, was a 17th century Carmelite monk who, after being crippled as a soldier in the Thirty Years' War between England and France, entered the monastery. He couldn't do much, so he was assigned to the kitchen to cook.

Despite his physical infirmity (which included continual pain) and his lowly job, he was a "gentleman of joyful spirit." His countenance revealed a sweet and calm devotion that affected all he encountered. Other monks asked him how and why he could maintain such joy in the midst of his circumstances. Brother Lawrence explained in a little pamphlet called *Practicing the Presence of God*.[99]

His "secrets" included the following recommendations:

1.) <u>Live in continual prayer.</u>

Brother Lawrence talked to God throughout every day and referred all he did to Him. He fed and nourished his soul with thoughts of God and His power, glory, and strength. To him the hours appointed for private prayer were no different, as far as being with God, than those he spent in the kitchen. Leaving "private prayer" time, he would pray:

"O my God, since Thou art with me, and I must now, in obedience to Thy commands, apply my mind to these outward things, grant me the grace to continue in Thy presence, and prosper me with Thy assistance. Receive all my works and possess all my affections."

2.) <u>Submit to God in all things and do all for the love of God.</u>

Brother Lawrence cautioned us to watch our passions and trust God to guide us about them. The love of God, he said, should be the purpose of all we do – not His gifts. Don't serve religion, he said, serve God.

Because he did everything in the kitchen for the love of God, he found the work there easy. Brother Lawrence believed, as Mother Teresa did, that God regards not the greatness of the work but the love with which it is performed.[100]

3.) <u>Shun attention and the limelight.</u>

Brother Lawrence said these were outside distractions and "spoiled all." The greatest pleasures of this world, he observed, are nothing compared to a spiritual state of constant fellowship with God.

4.) <u>Call upon God for strength and forgiveness.</u>

If Brother Lawrence was called upon to practice some virtue, he would call on God for strength. If he failed in his duty, he confessed his fault, and prayed, "If you leave me to myself this is all I can do. Hinder my failing and mind what is amiss." He believed we should pray to God about our affairs as they happened.

5.) <u>Have high regard and great esteem for God.</u>

The trust we put in God honors Him, counseled Brother Lawrence. Brother Lawrence trusted God to give him strength to endure any trial. He was ready to be a martyr (although he lived to be 81, a very old man in those days) so he feared nothing.

6.) <u>Pray for a sense of God's Presence.</u>

Brother Lawrence put the "Ask and you shall receive" principle to work.

7.) <u>Do your job, offer it to God, deny yourself.</u>

Be faithful in performing your job and deny yourself, said Brother Lawrence. Offer your work to Him and thank Him when you complete it. After a while unspeakable pleasures will follow.

Dr. Terry Teykl, a pastor, author, and widely sought-after speaker from Houston, Texas, says we should seek more of God's Presence in our churches, not more programs. He estimates 95 percent of American churches are program-based, not Presence-based. If our churches would only seek God's Presence, says Dr. Teykl, people would be drawn in, and church growth programs would not be necessary.[101] When God is center stage, people will know it. When He's not, the people will leave. The power will leave the church with the people.

One church that follows Dr. Teykl's advice is the Brooklyn Tabernacle in Brooklyn, New York, pastored by Jim Cymbala.

Cymbala says no matter where we are or what challenges we face, we cannot sustain a lifegiving ministry without a continual "baptism of love" from the Holy Spirit. Cymbala says he could not minister in the midst of the overwhelming problems he faces in the New York City area without it.

Cymbala came to Brooklyn Tabernacle, a church with under twenty members at that time, when he was 28. The first Sunday offering was $85. After two years without seeing much growth, he became ill and went to his in-laws' home in Florida to see if some rest would help. He had read many books on church growth, and one day in Florida while he was out fishing, he presented the ideas he had read about to God.

"Lord, what do I do? I'm in New York City with people dying all around me. You couldn't have put Carol and me here to do nothing. But God, how can we get their attention ... "

Then, Cymbala says, God spoke to him in the closest thing to an audible voice he has ever experienced. God told him if he and his wife would lead the people to pray and wait on Him, He would take care of every sermon, supply all the money they needed (both

When we seek God's presence, peace, power and provisions flow into our lives. personally and as a church) and bring in so many people that no building they used would be large enough to hold all the people.

Cymbala returned and told his congregation, "The barometer of our church is now going to be the prayer meeting. The key to our future as a church will be calling on God to release his miraculous power among us..."

At that time, Cymbala says, "We had about 15 people attending prayer meeting. [So] we began to wait on the Lord, and God gave us the gift of prayer. Worship and praise took hold. We saw that in direct proportion to the liberty God gave us in prayer, things happened: unsaved loved ones started getting converted ... People came in ... Spiritual power came through experiencing God's Presence, and God's Presence is found in sustained prayer."[102]

When we seek God's Presence, peace, power, and provision flow into our lives. When we focus on Him, He takes care of everything else. That's living abundantly.

Chapter 10

AN ABUNDANCE OF DEPENDENCE ON GOD

Very few of us know the time of our death, nor would we likely want to know if given the option. But if we knew and had the opportunity to talk to our family and dearest friends one last time, what would we say to them? We certainly wouldn't waste time talking about trivial things like yesterday's ball game or the weather report. We would focus on what *really* mattered, knowing this would be the last time on this side of heaven we could share our love and wisdom with those nearest and dearest to us.

Unlike most of us, Jesus knew when He was going to die. Before He took the disciples up to the last supper, He shared one final lesson with them – the one thing He knew they would need to remember. He had been with them for three years. But now, He would leave rash Peter, dense Philip, doubting Thomas, and the rest with the key that would enable them to carry on and succeed in spreading the gospel despite their limitations and weaknesses.

Jesus used a metaphor to convey His final message. He told His disciples that He was the vine, His Father the vinedresser. The disciples were the branches, and in order to produce fruit they had to stay connected to the vine. No branch, He told them, could bear fruit of itself. Only by staying vitally joined to the vine would any branch be able to produce. *"Dwell in Me, and I will dwell in you. [Live in Me, and I will live in you.],"* He said. *"Just as no branch can bear fruit of itself without abiding in (being vitally united to) the vine, neither can you bear fruit unless you abide in Me."* [103]

What was Jesus saying? That without Him the disciples couldn't catch fish, make tents, grow their crops? No. He was telling them that they could produce nothing of a true, godly, or spiritual nature that really glorified God without Him.[104]

Are we going to have an abundant life without total dependence on Jesus? Abundant lives produce lasting fruit. Jesus had just told the disciples they couldn't do it without their source.

What a Relief – We Don't Have to Do It Alone

Elisabeth Howard, a student at Wheaton College, fell in love with Jim Elliott, a graduate student with a heart for missions. They married and went to serve the Ouichua Indians in Ecuador. She shares how she had to learn to depend on God in the face of seemingly insurmountable odds – no Bible in the Ouichuan language, the mission station being washed away by a flood, and all their Ouichua language notes lost.

"One experience after another has to bring us to the point of stopping … God has to peel away all the layers until we realize we can't take our next breath without Him. When you have decided that what you really want is the kind of happiness God offers, when you have declared your dependence, then you must accept His strength for your weakness."

Elisabeth had to depend on the Everlasting Arms more than she ever imagined she would. She and Jim had just started a family when he and four other missionaries were out with the Ouichuan Indians and were brutally murdered because of a lie one of them had told the others about the missionaries' intent. Now, on top of everything else, Elisabeth was left without her husband and with a young daughter to support. And yet, despite her circumstances and great loss, she carried on – ministering there and showing the Indians the love of God.

She exhorts us, "I want you to think about this. What is your dependence? Christians are people who know they can't make it alone… What is the job God has asked you to do? Do you feel qualified? Are you prepared to obey? Do you think you're adequate for this job? You're not. That has nothing to do with whether or not you must be obedient. It's cooperation between you and Him to do the job in His strength. Declare your dependence."[105]

No Worries

We have relatives that live in the Australian Outback. My husband and I have been to Australia several times to visit. One of the Australians' favorite sayings is "No worries." We would say "No problem" in America, but its "no worries" there.

Jesus would favor the Australian version. He instructed us, in Matthew 6:25-27, not to worry:

"Therefore I tell you, stop being perpetually uneasy (anxious and worried) about your life, what you shall eat or what you shall drink; or about your body, what you shall put on. Is not life greater [in quality] than food, and the body [far above and more excellent] than clothing? Look at the birds of the air; they neither sow nor reap nor gather into barns, and yet your heavenly Father keeps feeding them. Are you not worth much more than they? And who of you by worrying and being anxious can add one unit of measure (cubit) to his

stature or to the span of his life?."

Have you ever been in a situation where you didn't worry about anything because whoever was in charge was so competent you knew everything would be fine? Worry would have simply caused unnecessary grief and loss of energy.

A few months ago I had outpatient surgery. I had so much confidence in the surgeon, I did not tell anyone except my immediate family. I knew everything would work out just fine, and I didn't want to bother my church friends and Bible study group because they would all be over with food. I wanted them to spend their energies in other ways. Had I not had total confidence in such an outstanding surgeon, I would have been very worried.

Under the anesthesia I was totally dependent. There was nothing I could do to help. I put myself in the surgeon's capable hands and he did a magnificent job.

Jesus tells us to be totally dependent on our heavenly Father, Who is far more compassionate, capable, and faithful than any person on earth. If He cares for the birds who don't worry, won't He even more so care for His own children? Each day the birds find food to sustain themselves. God provides internal guidance systems for them so they know when to fly to a new location to prepare for the changing seasons. What must the birds think of us? A little poem in a book I used to read, which goes something like this, comes to mind:

Said the robin to the sparrow,
"I wonder if you know
Why these anxious human beings rush about
And worry so?"

Said the sparrow to the robin,
"I think that it must be
They have no heavenly father such
As cares for you and me."

Freedom from worry means peace of mind, a necessary ingredient for an abundant life.

But how? How do we free ourselves from worry and depend on God when the diagnosis is cancer, or when we have no money in the bank and the creditors are calling, or when our teenage son or daughter has been picked up for illegal possession of drugs? Let me offer two suggestions that have helped me. Neither is original, but both have scriptural precedents.

Pray and Act Principle

The first is from Norman Vincent Peale, one of my virtual mentors. The secret of success, he says, is to work as if everything depends on us and pray as if everything depends on God. In other words, we all do whatever we can to make our situation better, but pray with all our hearts and minds to the one God, Who has all power to turn the situation around for us. What we do may be merely sybolic.

One of my favorite Bible stories is about Jehoshaphat, king of Judah, who faced the humanly impossible situation of having three enemy armies coming against him. Jehoshaphat's long strong suit was not defense. He had a puny army, but he was a wise and good ruler. He called his people together to pray and

Work as if everything depends on you and pray as if everything depends on God.

fast. As they were praying, a prophet among them stood up and said: *"Hearken, all Judah, you inhabitants of Jerusalem, and you King Jehoshaphat. The Lord says this to you: Be not afraid or dismayed at this great multitude; for the battle is not yours, but God's ... You shall not need to fight in this battle; take your positions, stand still, and see the deliverance of the Lord [Who is] with you, O Judah and Jerusalem. Fear not nor be dismayed. Tomorrow go out against them, for the Lord is with you.*" [106]

The next morning Jehoshaphat consulted with his people and then appointed the choir to lead his tiny army out to meet the enemy. The choir went out singing, "Give thanks to the Lord for His mercy and loving kindness endure forever."

Jehoshaphat did *something*. Although he knew his army was no match for the hordes coming against him, he took action and did what he knew to do.

Then God worked His miracle.

"*And when they began to sing and to praise, the Lord set ambushments against the men of Ammon, Moab, and Mount Seir who had come against Judah, and they were [self-] slaughtered;*"[107]

Pray and act. Expect God to deliver on His promises regardless of how meager your action is. After all, He cannot lie.[108]

The But God Principle

The second suggestion came to me through one of my actual mentors, Sue Bess, a precious 96-year-old lady who is a wonderful listener. When I was recently worried myself about a situation involving a former client who was upset and threatening to sue me, she gave me an article by Dr. V. Raymond Edman, former president of Wheaton College in Wheaton, Illinois.

In the article entitled "But God" [109] he reminds us that while we are to be realistic about our circumstances, we are also to remember God is above and beyond them. He quotes the psalmist, *"Lord how they are increased that trouble me! Many are they that rise up against me. Many there will be which say of my soul, There is no help for him in God ... But Thou, O Lord, art a shield for me; my glory, and the lifter up of mine head."*[110]

Believing prayer and physical rest, he continues, make us fearless in the Lord. "This is the divine antidote for fearfulness. God and one believer make a majority in any problem or perplexity."

We rest so we are not vulnerable to the attacks of the enemy. And we find a promise of God to pray, because we can believe God's promises. For example, if our problem is not enough money, we can pray "Lord, the creditors are calling every day. The stack of bills is getting higher and higher. I haven't made a mortgage payment in two months. My friends say I'll have to declare bankruptcy. But, You, O Lord, are a shield for me. You lift up my

Believing prayer and physical rest make us fearless in the Lord.

head. You cannot lie. You said in Your Word that if I would bring You the tithe, You would open the windows of heaven and pour me out a blessing so great I cannot take it in.[111] I now begin to tithe, claiming Your promise, and receiving your divine and miraculous provision so that I can pay *all* my bills.

We can take God's promise to the bank. As we claim and pray God's Word in our situation we *can* believe our prayer will be answered. The other part of the formula is easy – get plenty of rest.

"No soul can really be at rest until it has given up all dependence on everything else and has been forced to depend on the Lord alone," writes Hannah Whitehall Smith. "As long as our expectation is from other things, nothing but disappointment awaits us."[112]

Growth Through Dependence

The one thing we Christians get "right" is salvation. We

acknowledge there is absolutely nothing we can do to get saved in our own strength. Humanly, we cannot meet God's standard which is perfect righteousness.[113] We must have this attributed to us because no one except Jesus has ever been perfectly righteous. This happens when we receive Jesus as our Lord and Savior.[114] So, we readily admit we are totally dependent on Jesus for our salvation.

Where we miss the boat is to think we can obey God and grow spiritually in our own strength. I learned several years ago I could not obey God by forgiving a friend who had stabbed me in the back. I was too hurt and furious about what had happened. I began to pray that God would do the hard work for me. "Obey Yourself through me, God," I prayed, "I can't forgive him. I need You to do it for me." Do you think God will not answer a prayer to obey Himself?

What happened was one of the greatest miracles of my life. God took away all the bitterness and pain. He did not cause me to forget what happened. I remember it perfectly well, but it doesn't matter anymore. I have the same close relationship with my friend as I did before the painful experience. I could not have forgiven him, so I asked God to do it and He did!

Jesus taught, *"Blessed (happy, to be envied, and spiritually prosperous-- with life-joy and satisfaction in God's favor and salvation, regardless of their outward conditions) are the poor in spirit (the humble, who rate themselves insignificant), for theirs is the kingdom of heaven!"*[115] The word "poor" is translated from "ptochas" which means to "crouch or cower as one helpless." We must acknowledge our helplessness before God to grow spiritually.

Paul also taught that dependence is a blessing. *"So for the sake of Christ, I am well pleased and take pleasure in infirmities, insults, hardships, persecutions, perplexities and distresses; for when I am weak in human strength, then am I truly strong (able, powerful in divine strength)."*[116] He later adds, *"For though He was crucified in weakness, yet He goes on living by the power of God. And though we too are weak in Him as He was humanly weak, yet in dealing with you we shall show ourselves alive and strong in fellowship with Him by the power of God."*[117]

Without a sense of dependence and need we will not turn to Him. We will think we are sufficient in our own strength. Like Peter, who boasted to Jesus he would never desert Him, only to deny Him three times shortly thereafter, we will fall flat on our faces in spiritual failure. We grow spiritually largely by recognizing our own utter lack and turning to Him for strength, grace, wisdom, guidance, provision, healing, and peace.

We would do well to remember Jesus' last words to His inner circle of twelve, *"However, apart from Me ... you can do nothing.*[118]*"*

Chapter 11

AN ABUNDANCE OF DETERMINATION AND PERSISTENCE

*D*uring Lent this year, Bishop James R. King preached an inspiring sermon on living the abundant life Jesus came for us to live.

If God's Kingdom will come on earth, he said, all we are and all we are becoming will require great determination. "Life is movement and movement is life. We cannot be paralyzed by fear or pain. After surgery, our doctors want us to use our muscles again as soon as possible. We must keep moving to be well."

Discouragement is everywhere, he continued. Therefore we need something in us "greater than us" to go on. He shared some stories I had not previously heard. Michael Jordan, inducted into the basketball Hall of Fame, was cut from the basketball team in the ninth grade. Bill Cosby, one of the greatest comics ever to grace the American stage, failed the tenth grade *twice* before going on to get a Ph.D. in education. Arthur Blank, entrepreneur extraordinaire, was fired from his job at the hardware store before starting his own "little" hardware store known as The Home Depot.[119]

It's Worth the Effort

My wise mother used to tell me that anything really worth having or doing was going to be a lot of trouble. Anne Sullivan knew this.

The Miracle Worker[120] is the story of Anne Sullivan and the deaf and blind girl she tutored, Helen Keller. In the television adaptation of the drama, Helen's half-brother James is trying to get Anne ("Annie") to give up on Helen as all her other teachers had done. But Annie is determined. She remembers how her own brother had given up and died in a mental hospital. She and James talk:

James: "You don't let go of things easily, do you?"

Annie: "No. That's the original sin."

James: "What?"

Annie: "Giving up. Jimmie (Annie's brother) gave up."

James: "Perhaps Helen will teach you."

Annie: "What?"

James: "That there is such a thing as defeat. And no hope."
"And giving up. Sooner or later we do. Then maybe you'll have some pity on – all the Jimmies. And Helen, for being what she is. And even yourself."

(Annie sits for a moment and then gets up silently and turns and walks away from James. She paces for a few minutes in the semi-dark room and then walks over to the bed where Helen is sleeping. She drops to her knees at the bedside. The camera shows their faces: the sleeping child and the determined teacher.)

Annie: "No. I won't let you be. No pity. I won't have it. On either of us. If God didn't mean you to have eyes, I do. We're dead a long time. The world is not something to be missed. I know. And I won't let you be till I show you it. Till I put it in your head."

What would the *world* have missed (not to mention Helen) if Annie Sullivan had not been determined? If a couple of seemingly overwhelming obstacles, like blindness and deafness, had discouraged her? The student had great gifts that could be known only through the persistence of a courageous and dedicated teacher.[121]

Obstacles Are Tests

Dr. Randy Pausch, professor of computer science at Carnegie Mellon University, was forced into early retirement by a diagnosis of terminal pancreatic cancer. At Carnegie Mellon, retiring professors traditionally give a "last lecture," their final opportunity to impart their knowledge and wisdom to the students. Unlike all of their prior lectures, the last lecture does not have to be in their field of expertise, what they have taught at Carnegie Mellon. It can be about anything. If they want to talk about the joy of growing roses or how to improve a golf swing they are free to do so.

In his last lecture, a message so well received it turned into a book[122] and wound up on the *New York Times* bestseller list, Randy talked about how he reached his dream of becoming a professor of computer science at Carnegie Mellon. When he applied for admission as a graduate student at Carnegie Mellon, he was rejected. It took a call from one of his undergraduate professors to get him an interview, but from that point he talked his way in.   Disappointments, setbacks, and failures are there to test us to see how badly we want the goal we're aiming for, says Dr. Pausch. We can't let them discourage us. Keep going. If one road is blocked, find another one. Determination and persistence will clear the way. Our dreams can come true if we work hard and don't give up, he concludes.

Randy worked hard at his job, even after his doctors told him there was nothing else they could do for him. Through the preparation and delivery of his last lecture and the book it became, he provided inspiration for a nation and significant royalty income for his wife and three young children after he passed away. He never gave up but remained determined, to the last day he drew a breath.

Achieving Worthwhile Goals

Abundant Living means we will set and achieve worthwhile goals, the most significant of which will require power beyond our own to accomplish. Yes, we need Christ in us because we are sufficient in his sufficiency through the inner strength He provides.[123]

We may, however, be plodding along for a while doing everything we know to do and praying our hearts out thinking nothing is happening. John Hesselink, missionary to Japan, thought that. He was assigned the formidable task of teaching three Bible classes in the local prison by a veteran missionary about to leave on furlough. The veteran had been born in Japan and knew the language and culture well. John had been to language school but struggled with it, especially the biblical and theological vocabulary. Yet, he was assigned to teach the Bible to three groups of prisoners, most of whom knew nothing about the gospel. Two of the three groups were death row inmates.

Despite his well founded fears and apprehensions, John kept going back to the prison week after week. The setting was grim – a small, dark room with a somber-faced guard who sat off in a corner. His discouragement increased as winter set in, and the unheated rooms were even more depressing. He had the feeling at times he wasn't getting through as he tried to teach the New Testament with the aid of a translator. He had no chance to get to know the men because the guard quickly led them back to their cells immediately after each session. From their expressionless faces, he concluded he was a failure.

One day, however, something unusual occurred. He noticed after one class two men arguing with a guard. Suddenly the guard relented and said "OK" and three men approached John as the guard stood nearby. "Reverend Hesselink," they said, "for several months now we have been studying God's word with you. You have told us that God loves even condemned prisoners like ourselves, and that Jesus died for our sins and will forgive us if we repent and believe in him. We do believe this. We also have read that we must be baptized and confess that we trust him as our Savior. Will you baptize us?

Hesselink says he was stunned. All this time, he thought he wasn't getting through, but these men had come to understand the fundamentals of the gospel, even as presented by him with his limited, faulty Japanese. Christ had been at work in him, making his feeble efforts sufficient. All he had to do was keep showing up, regardless of how things looked.

When we know God's will, our job is to be persistent. God's job is to do the rest.

The director of the prison agreed to allow the three men to be baptized in his office and also agreed to allow a Japanese pastor to assist (Hesselink needed help reading the liturgy for the baptism). "What a glorious day that was when we gathered for that special service ... Their faith was sincere," he writes.

Hesselink concludes this testimony by reminding us of Zechariah 4:6: " *Not by might, nor by power, but by My Spirit..., says the Lord of hosts.*"[124]

When we know the goal is God's will, our job is to be persistent. God's job is to do the rest. He just needs us to stay available.

The PUSH Method of Prayer
(Pray Until Something Happens)

Perhaps nowhere is determination more important than in our prayer life. Jesus told a story of a certain widow who came to a corrupt judge seeking justice. The judge kept turning her away, but she was not deterred. Finally, though the judge cared nothing for her or for justice, he decided to defend, protect, and avenge her to gain peace for himself.

Jesus tells us to listen and learn from the unjust judge. If even a dishonest judge responds positively to one who refuses to take no for an answer, how much more will our just God respond to those who are determined to get their answer to prayer?[125]

Rev. Jimmy Swaggart tells a story about an illness he had as a 10-year-old child. He would get nauseated and then pass out. This happened several times at school. The doctors could not diagnose him, although they were able to rule out several illnesses. Jimmy's parents, his pastor, and many people at his church were praying for him to be healed, but apparently nothing was happening.

Finally, one day after an episode, the principal of his school told his parents that either something had to be done about his situation or they would have to take him out of school. "We don't want him to die here," the principal confided.

The next Sunday Jimmy, his parents, and his little sister were to take their pastor and his wife to dinner after church. But first they had to stop by the home of an ill member and pray for him. The pastor anointed the ill member with oil, prayed, and was about to leave when Jimmy's father said, "Pastor, would you pray for Jimmy again? If he is not healed, we are going to have to take him out of school."

"Of course," the kindly man said. He didn't say, "We've already done that; no need to pray again."

He approached Jimmy, put his thumb on Jimmy's forehead with the anointing oil, and prayed again for complete healing. Jimmy says with that prayer he felt a warmth about the size of his fist start at the top of his head and move through his body until it reached the bottom of his feet. He knew he had been healed. He didn't know why God waited until then to answer the prayer when it had been prayed so many times before but he experienced firsthand the power of persistent, determined prayer.

Since that day, Rev. Swaggart says he has enjoyed excellent health, travelling all over the world and never having any problems except for a two-hour bout with a bug somewhere in Brazil.[126]

What's Your Failure Quotient?

Abundant living means seeing our dreams come true. To succeed with a *big* dream will almost always require some failures and setbacks along the way. This is why it is so important for us to be determined to reach our goal and to keep pressing on even when circumstances look grim. There is much that is happening our limited human eyes are not able to see, and our determination and persistence move even God to come to our assistance.

Determination and persistence move even God.

I remember the story I heard once about a speaker at a

writer's conference awarding a prize (a copy of the book that was number one on the *New York Times* bestseller list) to the conference attendee who had received the most rejection slips from publishers. Her point was to branch out and try new things, even if it meant being rejected. She asked everyone who had received five rejection slips to stand. Many stood. After increasing the number of rejection slips received to a point where only one man was left standing, she declared him the winner and asked him to come forward. As he mounted the podium gasps could be heard all around the room. He was immediately recognized. The winner of the rejection slip contest was the author of the book being offered as the prize. Calvin Coolidge said it well:

> "Nothing in this world can take the place of persistence. Talent will not; nothing is more common than unsuccessful people with talent. Genius will not; unrewarded genius is almost a proverb. Education will not; the world is full of educated derelicts. Persistence and determination alone are omnipotent. The slogan "press on" has solved and always will solve the problems of the human race."

Chapter 12

AN ABUNDANCE OF INNER PEACE

*T*he local arts council decided to have a contest. They offered a prize to the artist who could best depict 'peace' in his or her painting. The community artists got busy. One painted a lake surrounded by mountains with a family of ducks paddling gently over the water's surface. Another entry featured a meadow full of wildflowers, with a doe and her fawn grazing undisturbed beside a pond. An elderly couple holding hands at the end of a summer day, facing a glorious sunset, was yet another submission.

But the winning entry was very different. A storm was raging. Lightning flashed across the canvas; heavy rain pelted the landscape; strong winds bent the trees.

Peace of mind is the gift that God reserves for his special protégés.

To the right there was a large oak tree with a nest. The mother bird held her strong wing over her chicks, protecting them from the ravages of the storm. Under her wing, the chicks slept soundly without a care in the world.

And isn't that the kind of peace we need to live abundantly?

We want peace no matter what the outward circumstances are. To know nothing can really hurt us is the peace for which we are longing, because sooner or later we are going to encounter something that rocks our boat.

What We Really Want

As a young man, Joshua Liebman made a list of everything he wanted in life: health, love, beauty, talent, power, riches, and fame. He was quite proud of his list and went to his mentor, an older and very wise gentleman, to show it to him. As the mentor reviewed the list, he looked thoughtfully at his protégé and said, "An excellent list, well digested in content and set down in not-unreasonable order. But it appears, my young friend, that you have omitted the most important element of all. You have forgotten the one ingredient lacking without which, each possession becomes a hideous torment, and your list as a whole, an intolerable burden."

"And what is that missing ingredient?" Joshua asked, a bit insulted.

The elderly man took a pencil stub and crossed out Joshua's entire list. Underneath he wrote three simple words: *peace of mind.* "This is the gift that God reserves for His special protégés," he said. "Talent and beauty He gives to many. Wealth is commonplace, fame not rare. But peace of mind – that is His final seal of approval, the fondest sign of his love."[127]

Joshua Liebman took his mentor's advice seriously and went on to write the book, *Peace of Mind,*[128] which sold over one million copies.

Peace Pilgrim

Whatever his name really is, he goes by Peace Pilgrim. Some might call him crazy, others an eccentric old man. But for those who seek, he is a messenger with a word of wisdom.

Peace Pilgrim has walked over 25,000 miles as a penniless pilgrim. He owns only what he wears and can carry is his small pockets. He walks until he is given shelter and fasts until he is given food. On the front of his tunic is a sign: "PEACE PILGRIM," on the back "25,000 miles on foot for Peace."

As he walks, he talks to those who approach him and shares his peace message:

"This is the way of peace: Overcome evil with good, falsehood with truth, and hatred with love."

In a radio interview, Peace Pilgrim said to his listening audience: "All of us can work for peace. We can work right where we are, right within ourselves, because the more peace we have within our own lives, the more we can reflect into the outer situation. ... So primarily my subject is peace within ourselves as a step toward peace in our world."

He then shared what he called "steps" to inner peace, noting that the order in which he presented them was not important because the first step for one could be the last step for another:

First, he says, we must have a right attitude toward life, a meaningful attitude for the problems life sets before us. Every problem that comes to us has a purpose and contributes to our inner growth. Problems, therefore, are opportunities in disguise and can contribute greatly toward our spiritual maturity (which occurs when we solve problems in accordance with the "highest light.")

Next, we must bring our lives into harmony with the laws of the universe. We must live the good things we believe in, not just give them lip service. If we are doing something we know to be wrong, we must stop doing it. And

Every problem that comes to us has a purpose.

if we know we are not doing something we should be doing, we must get busy doing it. The living should match the believing. As we live according to the highest light we have, other light will be given to us.

The third preparation is to discern our special place in God's plan. If we do not now know where we fit, says Peace Pilgrim, we should try seeking it in receptive silence. Walk on a beach, hike in the mountains, sit in a garden. Expect wonderful insights to come. If we do the good we know to do, giving it priority over the superficial things that clutter our lives, we will be shown our peace.

The final step, he says, is the simplification of life to bring inner and outer well-being into harmony. "Just after I dedicated my life to service, I felt I could no longer accept more than I needed while others in the world have less than they need. This moved me to bring my life down to need level. I thought it would be difficult. I thought it would entail a great many hardships but I was quite wrong … I discovered this great truth: unnecessary possessions are just unnecessary burdens … There is a great freedom in simplicity of living and after I began to feel this, I found a harmony in my life between inner and outer well-being."[129]

To summarize, he is saying we cannot feel and judge everything as it relates to us alone. We are all part of each other. We must always seek the good of *all*, not just what is right for us personally. While material things are there for us to use, when we no longer need them, we must be willing to give them up for someone else to use. Otherwise, we are

We must always seek the good of all.

possessed by our possessions and we are not free. We must also understand we do not possess any other human being, no matter how closely related that person may be. Only when we stop trying to run their lives can we live in harmony with them.

The relinquishment of negative feelings includes the relinquishment of worry. "Worry is a useless mulling over of things we cannot change," says Peace Pilgrim. "Let me mention one [way to avoid worry]. Seldom do you worry about the present moment; it's usually all right. If you worry, you agonize over the past which you should have forgotten long ago, or you're apprehensive over the future which hasn't even come yet. We tend to skim right over the present time. Since this is the only moment that one can have, if you don't live it you never really get around to living at all. If you do live this present moment, you tend not to worry. For me, every moment is a new opportunity to be of service."[130]

The man, whatever you might think of him otherwise, has tremendous insight.

The Quakers

The Quakers have long taught that inward peace is desirable, attainable, and the place from which all right action should originate.

In a paper entitled, "The Quaker Doctrine of Inward Peace,"[131] Howard H. Brinton begins by noting some of the reasons we lack inward peace – our busyness, different standards we encounter for the various areas of our lives (business, church, home, social class), and the general chaos in the world.

The Quaker way, he says, is to so order our inner lives that the outer pressures can be adequately met and dealt with, even as we increase inward tire pressure in a soft tire so it can better encounter the bumps on the road. For the Quaker, inner peace can be reached when all of God's immediate requirements, as understood, are faithfully met. As we are faithful to the light we have, more will be given. "Inner Peace comes through

Inner peace comes through obedience to the divine voice.

121

obedience to the Divine Voice as a friend complies with the wishes of his friend because the two are one spirit."[132]

Brinton quotes an 18th century Quaker by the name of Job Scott:

The one thing needful is real union with God, an actual joining with him in one spirit. Without this union let a man know what he will, believe, possess and enjoy whatever he may or can, but he is an alien and a wanderer on the earth. Nothing else can ever satisfy his soul or abidingly stay his mind. There is no other possible permanent rest for the sole of his foot. He may drive, toil and bustle about and many may think him in a state of enjoyment, but it is all a delusion. In the midst of all earths caresses, if he presumes to declare himself happy he does violence to truth and his own feelings and the truly wise are privy to the lie. If he professes religion, goes to meeting, practices the exteriors of devotion and talks much about faith and godliness, it may for a moment quiet his mind and deceive his soul and others but long he cannot rest composed without living in union with God. [133]

This makes perfect sense. If my husband and I are to live in unity, for example, sometimes one of us must surrender to the will and desire of the other for us to live in peace. God, unlike us, is perfect and His will is perfect. Therefore if there is a conflict (we want one thing and God wants another) we will not have peace until we surrender our will to His. Conflict in the soul arises from refusal to accept the truth. When we are in conflict with the higher God-centered will, our lower self-centered will simply seeks satisfaction in an area too limited to satisfy it.

As soon as we surrender to God's will, His peace floods in, and, along with the peace, comes the call to action without which that peace cannot continue.[134]

One of the methods Quakers use to achieve inner peace is getting on top of things. This simply means that while some problems cannot be solved on their own level, by achieving a higher, more inclusive experience, we can get above the problem. When this higher interest arises on the horizon, the lower, insoluble problem loses its urgency and is no longer important. Hence the conflict subsides because we are no longer in it, but above it.

If two children are fighting over a toy they cannot both play with at the same time and a parent comes forward and suggests they go to the store to get ice cream, the conflict immediately ceases. Now there is a broader, more inclusive experience at hand and the argument over the toy is forgotten.

The Gift of Peace

Jesus said, *"Peace I leave with you; My [own] peace I now give and bequeath to you. Not as the world gives do I give to you. Do not let your hearts be troubled, neither let them be afraid... "*[135]

Jesus is saying He will give us peace. We don't have to work for it. He wants to give it freely, but we must accept it even as we must accept any gift offered to us by anyone.

Dr. Charles L. Allen, author of *Life More Abundant,*[136] says in order to accept His peace, we must also accept three other things from Him: His pardon, His Presence, and His purposes.

We must accept His pardon because without that we will be haunted by a sense of guilt. We have all committed wrongs and, until we are forgiven, those sins will cause us to be uneasy. But God promises us cleansing as soon as we confess. *"If we [freely] admit that we have sinned and confess our sins, He is faithful and just (true to His own nature and promises) and will forgive our sins [dismiss our lawlessness] and [continuously] cleanse us from all unrighteousness [everything not in conformity to His will in purpose, thought, and action].*"[137]

We are, however, also required to forgive others to accept His pardon. Jesus said if we forgive other people their trespasses against us, our heavenly Father will forgive us.[138]

As long as we hold bitterness in our hearts against one of our fellow human beings, we have no room for God. Nor will God's loving mercy and our unforgiving spirit "mix." Like oil and water, the two substances (spiritual in this case) simply aren't going to mesh.

In fact, nothing robs us of peace more than an unforgiving, judgmental spirit. Maybe we were wronged. Maybe 100 out of 100 people would agree that we were the victims in a given situation. The person that hurt us is not the least bit repentant. Why should we forgive? Even apart from God's promise of forgiveness as we forgive others, forgiveness frees us. Once we make up our minds to forgive in this situation we no longer carry around the baggage of bitterness, resentment, anger, or hatred. We are now able to receive peace because we've gotten rid of what doesn't mix with it. As my friend Becky says, "Forgiveness is a gift you give yourself."

> **As long as we hold bitterness in our hearts against one of our fellow human beings, we have no room for God.**

The second thing we must accept before we can accept His peace, says Dr. Allen, is His Presence.[139] In England during World War II, the authorities evacuated the children from areas under bombardment. Although the children were safe and all of their physical needs were met, they became very upset emotionally by being away from their parents.

And so it is with us. We may have everything we need

physically, even at the most luxurious level, but if we are not living in the Presence of God, enjoying His fellowship, we are not going to be able to accept His peace.

As the great prophet Elijah learned, we find His Presence in the stillness. Elijah was on the run from Queen Jezebel, who had threatened to kill him. He was complaining that only he was left, of all the Israelites, to worship God. God directed him to stand on the mountain before Him. As Elijah stood there, a powerful wind passed by breaking rocks into small pieces, *"but the Lord was not in the wind."* After the wind there was an earthquake, *"but the Lord was not in the earthquake."* Next, came a fire, *"but the Lord was not in the fire."*[140] After the fire came a gentle stillness and a still, small voice. When Elijah heard the still, small voice, he recognized it as the voice of God.[141]

To experience God's Presence we must be still in body and mind.[142]

Finally, we must accept God's purpose. This, as the Quakers teach, means accepting God's will and relinquishing our will to His.

The great poet Dante wrote, "In His will is our peace."

Chapter 13

AN ABUNDANCE OF GRATITUDE

Corrie Ten Boom, in her book *The Hiding Place,* tells about her experience in a German concentration camp during World War II. She and her family had hidden Jews from the Germans and were hauled off to pay for their "sins." In the camp, the Christians would gather together in a flea-infested hut to pray and study what little part of the Bible they were able to bring with them. The fleas were a nuisance, making a terrible situation even worse. As the women prisoners gathered to study and pray, they naturally complained about these pesky annoyances. But then, someone remembered a verse of Scripture commanding us to thank God in everything, no matter what the circumstances, because that was God's will for us. (I Thess. 5:18). In obedience, the women began thanking God for their flea-infested place of worship even though they had no idea *why* they were thankful. The study and fellowship were precious and sweet to them – the one bright spot in an otherwise desolate existence.

After the war ended, Corrie encountered one of the prison camp guards who had since given her life to Christ. She asked why the guards allowed the prisoners to read the Bible and pray together during their time in the concentration camp. Corrie thought the Germans would have broken that up from the onset. The former guard laughed, explaining none of them wanted to go into that flea-infested place where they gathered to study and pray. They chose their own comfort over ensuring the prisoners were conforming to camp rules. Corrie then saw the fleas as God's chosen means of warding the guards off so His daughters could gather together with Him for strength and encouragement, and finally understood why they had been thanking God for what they perceived to be an added burden. The fleas, it turned out, were a blessing.

It's easy to be grateful when everything is going our way. God has answered our prayer for that promotion, we just got a clean bill of health from the doctor, travelling mercies were given for a long trip to a third world country, someone we prayed for received Christ, our child found the perfect soon-to-be spouse, and we are delighted. Everything is going our way – why shouldn't we be grateful?

But sooner or later, something will not be to our liking. In fact, sooner or later, something a lot worse than fleas will hit us, and we may actually or figuratively shake our fist at God and ask, "Why? What have I done to deserve *this*? Where *were* You when this happened? How could You have *let* this happen?"

And, yet, the Bible says, "Be thankful *in* everything." (note: not *for* everything). And if we belong to God through Christ Jesus, and are called according to His purpose, we know that *all* things are working together and fitting into a plan for our good.[143]

As the women in Corrie's prayer group thanked God, He took those little insects and used them to protect the most precious thing the women had. Who knows – as the women gave thanks, God could have magnified flea power in the minds of the German guards, causing them to think of the insects as much more menacing and dangerous than they actually were.

The Power of Gratitude

We usually think of gratitude or thankfulness as a blessing we confer on others because they have done something to help or benefit us. Our mothers taught us to say "thank you" and even to write thank you notes if we received special benefits. It was just the way to operate in polite society. Not observing the social niceties would have repercussions – we would be viewed as ungrateful, lazy, selfish.

The Bible, however, tells us to be grateful to God in *all* circumstances because, no matter how grim things look, He is working them out for good for those who love Him.

Let's look at one of the humanly impossible situations Jesus faced. Jesus, Matthew's gospel tells us, had gotten word that His cousin John the Baptist had been beheaded, and He went away by boat to be alone in a "solitary" place. The crowds followed Him to this remote location to be healed and hear His teaching.

The Bible tells us to be grateful to God in all circumstances.

There were no *Mickey D's* around the corner; no hot dog vendors ready to sell food, water, cookies, suntan lotion, and snow cones to the hungry followers. To eat, the crowd would have to disperse and go home without their needs being met.

Jesus did not want them to go, but He knew their physical needs had to be met before He could minister to them at a deeper level. The disciples found a boy willing to give up the sack lunch his mother had prepared for him – five loaves and two fish. Jesus took the loaves and fish and ordered the crowds[144] to sit down. Then He prayed.

Now if I had been in that situation I would probably have prayed for a miracle, focusing on the meager amount of food I had to feed so many people. I would have told God how hungry they were, how desperately we needed Him to send a caravan over the hill laden with enough supplies to feed all the hungry people.

But what did Jesus pray? He simply looked up to heaven and gave thanks for the loaves and fish. Jesus did not focus on what He didn't have. He was grateful for what He *did* have. And, God provided. God increased the loaves and fish so that the thousands of people who came to hear Jesus preach ate and were satisfied. In fact, they picked up 12 small handbaskets full of broken pieces left over.[145]

Grateful People Are Healthier, Happier People

Two eminent psychologists, Dr. Robert A. Emmons and Dr. Michael E. McCullough, published a paper in the *Journal of Personality and Social Psychology* reporting the results of research they did on the effect of a grateful outlook on psychological and physical well-being.[146]

These two experts found that gratitude plays a significant role in a person's sense of well-being. While pastors, priests, rabbis, parents, and grandparents have long encouraged gratitude as a positive force in our lives, until recently scholars have ignored it.

McCullough and Emmons conducted a research project involving hundreds of people, dividing them into three groups. Group One was instructed to keep a diary of events that occurred during the day; Group Two was told to keep a diary of unpleasant experiences that occurred to them; and Group Three made a daily list of things for which they were gratful.

The results of the study indicated that daily gratitude

exercises resulted in higher reported levels of alertness, enthusiasm, determination, optimism, and energy. The gratitude group also experienced less depression and stress, was more likely to help others, exercised more regularly, and made more progress toward personal goals. Emmons and McCullough also found people who felt grateful were more

Gratitude plays a significant role in a person's sense of well-being.

likely to feel loved, and they noted that gratitude encouraged a positive cycle of reciprocal kindness among people, since one act of gratitude encourages another. Anyone, they concluded, could increase their sense of well-being and create positive social effects just by counting their blessings.

Clinical psychologist Blair Justice, professor emeritus of psychology at the University of Texas School of Public Health at Houston, says, "A growing body of research supports the notion that rediscovering a sense of abundance by thinking about those people and things we love lowers the risks of coronary events. At the end of the day, I ask myself three questions:

- What has surprised me?
- What has touched me?
- What has inspired me?"

Justice believes these three questions can improve our health by helping us to see the stuff of our days through fresh eyes.[147]

Practicing Gratitude

Life coaches and authors writing in the self-help genre have suggested several good ways to practice gratitude. Let me share a few:

1) <u>Keeping a gratitude journal</u>. This consists of writing down, at the beginning or end of each day, at least three things for which we are grateful.

2) <u>Writing a gratitude letter</u>. This is a letter written to someone who has exacted a positive influence in our lives but whom we have not properly thanked. We can even arrange a meeting to read the letter to his special person ourselves. Perhaps it is a grandparent or favorite aunt or a teacher. All of us have someone who has influenced us in positive ways that we haven't told.

3) <u>Find a tangible object to look at daily to remind us to stop complaining</u>. (The converse, of course, is to *start* being grateful.) Perhaps a special bracelet for women and a lapel pin for men.

4) <u>Fake it 'til you make it</u>. Say "thank you" even when we don't feel like it. Sooner or later our minds will fall in line with our words.

5) <u>Say grace before meals</u>.

6) <u>Keep a gratitude box</u>. In this box we can place photos, notes, gratitude lists, and notes we want to keep. (Note: one of my friends recently received such a box from her granddaughter for her 50th wedding anniversary. This friend's granddaughter had written her and her husband a sweet note, thanking them for the powerful influence they had been in her life and suggesting they use the box to keep other mementos of the wonderful life they have lived and continue to live. No $100,000 gift would have meant more to my friend than that precious note.)

7) <u>Send a card or email to someone you appreciate.</u>

8) <u>Write a thank you letter to God.</u> He can read, you know!

9) <u>Even if you don't write it down, take a few minutes at the end of each day to reflect on the good things that happened and why they were good.</u> It can be simple things like "Jenny made her bed today without me reminding her" or "Carolyn bent over backwards to help me with that rush job at work" or "Carl told me he liked my new dress."

10) <u>Want what you have.</u>

Levels of Gratitude

Many self-help gurus propound the Law of Attraction, which holds we attract into our lives what we admire, praise, and are grateful for. If we are grateful for the small amount of wealth we have, for example, we will attract more wealth.

Self-help guru Steve Pavlina however, warns there is an effective and an ineffective way to practice gratitude. He says he was stuck in the ineffective way for 10 years before he finally broke out of his noose and discovered the effective way to be grateful. He calls the ineffective way Level One Gratitude and the effective way Level Two Gratitude. Note, however, even Level One Gratitude has significant benefits as Doctors Emmons and McCullough discovered. What Steve Pavlina is talking about is being grateful in a way that attracts the things we want into our lives, or using gratitude to trigger the Law of Attraction.[148]

Level One Gratitude is gratitude for our possessions and immediate circumstances. We are grateful for our family, our job, our health, our home, our friends, our church, a vacation coming up.

Pavlina says while there's nothing wrong with Level One Gratitude, people often use it as a quick fix when they are actually feeling negative or complacent about their circumstances and trying to build some positive momentum. They don't feel genuinely grateful because ultimately their circumstances just aren't that exciting. This level of gratitude, Pavlina advises, is simply too weak to trigger the Law of Attraction.[149] It is dependent on circumstances, and when a negative circumstance hits, it can jolt us right out of an attitude of gratefulness.

Level Two Gratitude, on the other hand, is independent of situations and circumstances. It's the kind of gratitude St. Paul talked about when he said, *"Not that I am implying that I was in any personal want, for I have learned how to be content (satisfied to the point where I am not disturbed or disquieted) in whatever state I am."*[150] It's a feeling of gratitude for life itself and for everything life has to offer. It goes beyond Level One Gratitude to include being grateful for the opportunity to be alive, as well as problems, challenges and hardships, mistakes, unpleasant people we encounter, aches and pains, thoughts and emotions, and ideas and concepts. The underlying theme of Level Two Gratitude is "How wonderful it is to exist!"[151] We are fascinated with the very idea of life, with its twists and turns, fortunes and challenges, experiences and encounters. When we look back and see where we've been, we can say "What a ride!" Every experience is a WOW experience.

Does this take practice? You bet. But look at the payoff.

Pavlina makes an analogy of playing a state-of-the-art video game. We are amazed by the graphics, music, characters, and game play. It doesn't matter so much whether we win or lose as the fact we get to play the game. The experience is what counts. If we keep playing, we'll get good at it and eventually win, but it's fun even when we're not winning because we're having fun just playing.

When we move into Level Two Gratitude, gratitude becomes a part of who we are. We no longer say "I am grateful for ..." We just say "I am grateful."

This, Pavlina says, is the kind of magnetic gratitude that attracts the good things we want. Gradually, he says, his life circumstances changed with increased income, better relations with his kids, and more influence.

To get to a Level Two Gratitude state, Pavlina suggests we begin by consciously being grateful for things we wouldn't normally be grateful for – the bushes in our yard, the state workers painting new lines on the highway, our breathing. Then select something we would normally be ungrateful for (for example, an argument we had with our neighbor Sam). Hold the thought, "I am grateful for the argument I had with Sam." Sooner or later we will begin to see some good or beauty coming out of that event. Eventually, we will shift toward an unconditional feeling of gratitude.[152]

Consider:

1) If St. Paul had not gone to jail, he would likely not have had time to write the letters that make up so much of our New Testament.

2) If Joseph had not been sold into slavery, he never would have been a ruler in Egypt, able to save his family from the famine.

3) If Daniel had not been thrown into the lions' den, we never would have seen the miracle of God's deliverance (and we can say this about many seemingly impossible situations).

4) If Jesus hadn't gone to the cross, we could never have had our sins wiped away.

As Joseph told his brothers, *"…You thought evil against me, but God meant it for good."*[153]

As we remember that God works all things together for good for those who love Him and are called according to His purpose,[154] isn't it only logical to live in an attitude of gratitude? Henry Ward Beecher, one of the most effective and influential Protestant spokesmen of the 19th century, said it well:

> If one should give me a dish of sand, and tell me there were particles of iron in it, I might look for them with my eyes and search for them with my clumsy fingers, and be unable to detect them; but let me take a magnet and sweep through it and how it would draw to itself the almost invisible particles by the mere power of attraction. The unthankful heart, like my finger in the sand, discovers no mercies; but let the thankful heart sweep through the day, and as the magnet finds the iron, so it will find, in every hour, some heavenly blessing. Only the iron in God's sand is gold.[155]

Chapter 14

AN ABUNDANCE OF JOY

$\mathcal{T}$he party was in full swing. Everyone was having a grand time – the host and hostess had spared no expense to make sure the wedding reception would be the talk of the town for months. Among the guests joining in the celebration on His friends' most important day was Jesus of Nazareth, and what a glorious occasion this was. The guests were laughing, chatting, telling stories about the bride and groom, and enjoying the feast. Suddenly, however, a problem developed. Mary, Jesus' mother, a close family friend, realized the wine was all gone. How embarrassing it would be for the host and hostess to run out on one of the most important days of their lives, when they had invited all their friends to the festivities.

Mary found Jesus and informed Him there was no more wine. Jesus indicated He would take care of it, sparing the host and hostess humiliation. He had the servants fill six water pots (about 20-30 gallons each) with water, which they did.

He then instructed them to draw some out and take it to the manager of the feast. When the manager tasted Jesus' wine, he was amazed, saying to the bridegroom, "Everyone else serves his best wine first, and when people have drunk freely, then he serves that which is not so good, but you have kept back the good wine until now!"[156]

With this miracle, Jesus began His public ministry. A miracle of helping people rejoice. And, why not? God had appointed special times for His people to set aside for celebration and remembrance. The Israelites celebrated Passover, Pentecost, and the Feast of the Tabernacles, special days to remember God's blessings and deliverances.

We all need times of joy, refreshing, and remembrance to live abundantly. Can you imagine what it would be like never to go to a party, or celebrate birthdays and Christmas, or take a vacation?

This is not frivolous. Joy has an important purpose in our lives. Without times of refreshment and joy, we can get stressed out, burned out, worn out, and we can drop out. God knows we need balance.

Catalysts of Joy

One author defines joy as "a spirit of celebrating life, of delighting in all God has bestowed on us. It means to enjoy our days, to take genuine pleasure in them, notwithstanding what those days might hold".[157]

Some people are naturally joyful. We love to be around them because they help us laugh and have fun. Others are not. I heard a preacher on television recently say, "When I first started preaching, I had a problem. I know I was saved. If I had died back then, I would have gone to heaven, but I sure wouldn't have taken anybody with me. My attitude was awful." I'm sure this preacher is right. With a down attitude, we turn people away. A happy, joyful spirit attracts others.

Accepting God's forgiveness opens the door to joyful living.

But, if we are not naturally joyful, how do we cultivate it? (Remember, joy is one of the fruits of the Holy Spirit in Galatians 5:22-23).

Michael Zigarelli, dean of the Business School at Regent University, conducted a survey of over 5,000 Christians around the world. By comparing Christians who are consistently joyful with those who have less joy, he identified four primary catalysts of joy.

First, people who are confident their sins have been forgiven are more joyful than those who are not. Accepting God's forgiveness opens the door to joyful living. Perhaps some of these Christians have not forgiven themselves and, because of that, don't see how God can forgive them. But we should remember God is much greater and more able than we are and by accepting His forgiveness, we can know our eternal destiny is sure.[158]

The first catalyst lays the foundation for the second, which is forgiving others. Those who said they "always" forgave others, Zigarelli found, reported twice as much joy as those who said they "never" forgave others. And, in between, he reported, was a steady, growing relationship between forgiveness and joy. This makes sense. Refusal to forgive breeds anger, bitterness, and resentment, enemies of joy. Consciously choosing to forgive removes these obstacles.

Gratitude spawns joy.

The third catalyst for consistent joy is feeling life has real purpose. Psychologists, he notes, tell us that joy is a by-product of goal attainment and that mastery of a task or intellectual pursuit can be a stimulus for joy. As Pearl S. Buck said, "The secret of joy in work is contained in one word – excellence. To know how to do something well is to enjoy it."[159]

Finally, Zigarelli found that gratitude spawns joy. Grateful people are incessantly focused on what they have, not what they don't have. They ignore the Joneses and all the others who are trying to keep up with them. By *not* focusing on what's missing, they find joy in the blessings they are constantly counting. Someone asked World War I hero Eddie Rickenbacker, who was afloat on a raft in the Pacific Ocean hopelessly lost for 21 days before being rescued, what he had learned from the experience. Mr. Rickenbacker replied, "If you have all the fresh water you want to drink and all the food you want to eat, you ought never to complain about anything."[160]

Zigarelli concludes by saying that while God wants us to enjoy our lives, there is more at stake than that. Joy is not an end in and of itself. In joy and celebration we enable other virtues God wants to cultivate in us and great strength to do His will. "Restoring joy to our lives is also a pathway to consistent Christian living – to authentic witness, to a closer relationship with God, and to blessing abundantly everyone around us."[161]

Joy Boosters

British writer G.K. Chesterton called joy the "gigantic secret" of God and the "serious business of heaven" and, he continued, it should also be the serious business of our lives and ministry.[162]

C.S. Lewis believed that joy was quite opaque to evil and the evil one because all evil is baffled and offended by the essence of joy.[163]

These two great thinkers understood the importance of consciously allowing ourselves to be refreshed. Even as the Psalmist writes in the 23rd Psalm, lying down in green pastures, beside still waters, restoring our souls, is a blessing.

There are many ways to refresh ourselves because each of us is made differently and responds differently. I have a friend in ministry who unwinds by watching old TV westerns.

With the help of John Wayne, Gene Autry, Roy Rogers, and Dale Evans, she finds strength to go back to her work as a chaplain at the Atlanta airport.

Many of us unwind by spending time with friends and family around the dinner table. I have one friend who brings an item of interest from the newspaper to dinner to ask his fellow diners what they think of it. It might be an article on stem cell research or on some environmental issue. It gets the conversation going and helps us learn more about each other.

In the movie *Julie and Julia*, a young stressed-out career girl working in New York finds great release by trying every recipe in Julia Child's cookbook in a one-year time period, blogging about it as she goes. At one point in the movie, she says "Julia saved me." Her new hobby (French cooking) took her mind off of all the problems at work and enabled her to go back refreshed each day. Hobbies are wonderful ways of finding joy.

Golf, bridge, chess, reading, fishing, running, going to the gym, tennis, racquetball, softball, boating, skiing, biking, soccer, and every other physical and mental activity imaginable are ways we unwind and bring joy back into our lives. And just listening to music or watching a good movie will do the trick for some us as well.

We all need to find out what works for us, and make sure we've consciously scheduled time for that activity as an important part of our day.

Finding Joy in the Midst of Pain

The prophet Habakkuk said it well: *"[17]Though the fig tree does not blossom and there is no fruit on the vines, though the product of the olive fails and the fields yield no food, ...Yet will I rejoice in the Lord; I will exult in the victorious God of my salvation.*

[19]The Lord God is my strength, my personal bravery, and my invincible army; He makes my feet like hinds' feet and will make me to walk...and make spiritual progress upon my high places of trouble, suffering, or responsibility. "*[164]*

Thelma Wells, author of *God Is Not Through With Me Yet*, was diagnosed with cancer and spent several days in intensive care on life support, not expected to live. Her family was called in to say goodbye. But God, she says, had other plans and walked through that experience with her. When she looks back and sees what He did, her joy builds.

Thelma reports that as a young wife and mother she tried to be all things to all people and found herself burned out and miserable. Slowly, she realized she couldn't keep up the pace and started thinking and praying about who she really was and what her priorities should be. She found that God was secondary in her life, and she hadn't even seen it because she had just been too busy.

She learned to do what she called reality checks. She would tell herself she wasn't in control – God was. And she started taking her problems to Him – praying about them and searching Scriptures to find out how to deal with them. Every day she would pray, "Lord, you direct my path today. Open the doors I need to walk through. Close the doors I don't. Get people out of my way I don't need to talk to today. And put people in my path I do. And, Lord, don't let me waste time. For I trust you with everything."

The source of joy is our creator God.

Thelma found that as she focused on who she was in Christ, God began to restore her joy. It was a process; she says, and involved working through emotionally, physically, and spiritually the dilemma she had put herself in. But when she understood who she truly was and what God wanted to do in and through her life, He rejuvenated her and restored her joy.[165]

Another woman, Miriam, suffered from Huntington's disease, a genetic disorder. The disease was moving very slowly in her body and her doctors were amazed, telling her the symptoms were reduced by 50 percent over those of a normal patient. Miriam's attitude is reflected by two thoughts on her refrigerator:

"In the world you will have trouble but be of good cheer, I have overcome the world;"[166] and,

"Lord, if you can't make me thin, make my friends look fat!"

Miriam's strong faith and sense of humor in the midst of her disease helped her fight it.

Facets of Joy

Joy can be quiet or exuberant, renew energy and cure fatigue, clear the air so we can see things more accurately, free us from fears, and restore our souls. We need it to live abundantly.

The source of joy is our creator God. Evil cannot understand joy as C.S. Lewis so beautifully discusses in his chapter on laughter in *The Screwtape Letters*. As Screwtape, the senior devil, says to his mentee, Wormwood, "[Joy] is of itself disgusting and a direct insult to the realism, dignity and austerity of Hell."[167]

Why shouldn't we, as Christians, be joyful? All the heavy, serious stuff was dealt with at the cross. Death was swallowed up in victory. Eternal life was promised through our relationship with Christ and we know the end of the story – and it's an ending far better than we could have ever dreamed.

Rejoice and Live Abundantly!

End Notes

[1] John 10:10.

[2] Nina Munteanu, *The Fiction Writer* (Delta, BC Canada: Pixl Press, 2008), 94.

[3] Psalm 23:4(a).

[4] John 15:4-5.

[5] http://thinkexist.com/quotation/we-cannot-do-great-things-on-this-earth-only/488037.html.

[6] e.g., Psalm 37:4, Amos 4:13, Matthew 14:27, John 17:1.

[7] Jeremiah 29:11, "For I know the thoughts and plans that I have for you, says the Lord, thoughts and plans for welfare and peace and not for evil, to give you hope in your final outcome."

[8] Jane Johnson Struck, "Becoming a Purpose-Filled Woman," *Today's Christian Woman*. http://www.christianitytoday.com/tcw/2006/janfeb/8.42.html.

[9] Kathleen Doheny, "Have Purpose in Life? You Might Live Longer," *Health Day Reporter*, June 16, 2009. http://news.health.com/2009/06/16/have-purpose-life-you-might-live-longer/.

[10] "Having a Higher Purpose in Life Reduces Risk of Death Among Older Adults," *Medical News Today*, June 16, 2009. http://www.medicalnewstoday.com/articles/154016.php.

[11] "How to Know Your Life Purpose Plus How You Can Make a Big Difference." http://www.relfe.com/life_purpose.html.

[12] Id.

[13] Malcolm Gladwell, *The Outliers* (New York: Little, Brown and Co., 2008), 71.

[14] Gladwell, 110.

[15] Gladwell, 93.

[16] Gladwell, 94.

[17] Henry Alford, "The Keepers of Wisdom – What the stories of old people tell us about ourselves," Book Page, (*America's Book Review*, January 2009), 15.

[18] John 13:1-17.

[19] John 8:3- 11.

[20] Luke 10:38-42.

[21] John 15:1-17.

[22] Hebrews 7:25.

[23] Bob Benson, Sr. and Michael W. Benson, *Disciplines for the Inner Life*, (Nashville: Thomas Nelson Publishers, 1989), 224-225.

[24] Denise Lones, "The Importance of Mentors and Role Models." http://realtytimes.com/rtpages/20080916_mentors.htm.

[25] Jennifer Thomson, "The Role and Importance of Mentors." http://www.agora.forwomeninscience.com/education_of_girls_ and_women/2006/03/the_role_and_importance_of_men.php.

[26] Pat Boone, *Pray to Win: God Wants You to Succeed* (New York: G.P. Putnam and Sons, 1980).

[27] 3 John 1:2.

[28] Id.

[29] 1 Timothy 6:6-10.

[30] Matthew 6:19.

[31] 2 Corinthians 9:8.

[32] David Van Biema and Jeff Chu, "Does God Want You to be Rich?" *Time* magazine, September 18, 2006.

[33] 1 Chronicles 29:12.

[34] Isaiah 23:18.

[35] Matthew 25:13-29.

[36] J. Gilchrist Lawson, *Deeper Experiences of Famous Christians* (Anderson: Warner Press, 1911), 190-204.

[37] Ben Smith, "Sermons on Obama to go into Archives," *The Atlanta-Journal Constitution*, 5 January 2009, A1.

[38] "progress," *Random House Dictionary of the English Language, Unabridged*, 2nd Ed. (New York: Random House, 1987), 1546.

[39] Tracy, Brian, "The Ultimate Goals Program," Simon and Schuster Audio, a Nightingale-Conant Production, 2003.

[40] Fred A. Wolf, *Taking the Quantum Leap* (New York: Harper and Rowe, 1989), 185, 186-188.

[41] Tracy, "Ultimate Goals Program."

[42] Id.

[43] Richard C. Stazesky, "George Washington, Genius in Leadership,"

The Papers of George Washington Articles, February 22, 2000. http://gwpapers.virginia.edu/articles/stazesky.html.

[44] Exodus 15:20-27.

[45] Ann Spangler, *Praying the Names of God* (Grand Rapids: Zondervan, 2004), 100.

[46] Isaiah 40:31.

[47] Psalm 34:20.

[48] 3 John 1:2.

[49] Isaiah 55:11.

[50] Proverbs 18:21.

[51] James 5:15.

[52] Jim Glennon, *Your Healing Is Within You* (South Plainfield: Bridge Publishing, 1978), 19-21.

[53] James 1:6-7.

[54] 2 Kings 3:1-17.

[55] 2 Kings 3:20.

[56] Maxwell Maltz, *Psycho-Cybernetics* (Englewood Cliffs: Prentice-Hall, 1960), 35.

[57] Shakti Gawain, *Creative Visualization* (Novato: Nataraj Publishing, 1978), 79.

[58] 2 Corinthians 12:8-10.

[59] Michael J. Fox, *Always Looking Up: The Adventures of an Incurable Optimist*, (New York: Ebiery Press – a division of Random House, 2009).

[60] Charles L. Allen, *God's Psychiatry* (Old Tappan: Fleming H. Revell Co., 1953).

[61] Bubonic plague, Wikipedia, March 18, 2009 http://en.wikipedia.org/wiki/Bubonic_plague

[62] Oberammergau Passion Play, Wikipedia, http://en.wikipedia.org/wiki/Oberammergau_Passion_Play

[63] 2 Kings 3:20-24.

[64] 2 Chronicles 20.

[65] Isaiah 59:2.

[66] Daniel 3:25.

[67] Esther 5-9.

[68] 2 Chronicles 20.

[69] Sarah Young, *Jesus Calling: Enjoying Peace in His Presence* (Brentwood: Integrity Publishers, 2004), 79.

[70] "Finding the Eye of the Storm," Interview with Pastor Craig Barnes, *Leadership*, January 1, 1998. http://www.ctlibrary.com/le/1998/winter/811020.html.

[71] Exodus 16:15.

[72] Matthew 17:27.

[73] Mark 6:38-43.

[74] Cothern, Clark, "Tough Times, Tough Questions," *Leadership*, April 1, 1996. http://www.ctlibrary.com/le/1996/spring/612031.html.

[75] Adaptation: John Newton, *Amazing Grace*, c. 1772.

[76] "Student Is Billionaire Overnight," Skynews, October 23, 2008. http://news.sky.com/skynews/Home/World-News/Moldova-Student-Sergey-Sudev-Inherits-Nearly-A-Billion-Euros-From-Long-Lost-Uncle-In-Germany/Article/200810415126833.

[77] Stephen J. Kunitz and Irena Pesis-Katz, "Mortality of White Americans, African Americans and Canadians: The Causes and Consequences for Health of Welfare State Institutions and Policies." The Milbank Memorial Fund, 2005. http://www.milbank.org/quarterly/8301feat.html.

[78] Miranda Hitti, "Life Expectancy Reaches New Record," WebMD, November 11, 2008. http://www.webmd.com/news/20080611/life-expectancy-reaches-new-record.

[79] John 10:10.

[80] Galatians 3:28.

[81] James D. Hester, *Paul's Concept of Inheritance, a contribution to the understanding of Heilsgeschischte* (Edinburgh: Oliver and Boyd, 1968), 10 -11.

[82] John 14:8-9.

[83] Luke 24:10.

[84] I Timothy 2:12.

[85] John 14:15 -16 and John 16:7.

[86] Augustine, *The City of God* (New York: Random House Inc., 1950), 840, 861.

[87] Augustine, 864-867.

[88] Max Lucado, *Just Like Jesus*, (Nashville: Thomas Nelson, 1998), 135.

[89] Revelation 21:21.

[90] John 14:2-3.

[91] 1 Chronicles 29:11.

[92] Matthew 16:19-20.

[93] Hebrews 3:5.

[94] Psalm 16:11.

[95] Richard Wurmbrand, *Tortured for Christ* (Bartlesville: Living Sacrifice Book Company, 1967), 94.

[96] Psalm 18:1 and 18:16.

[97] Atha Grayson, "Learning to See God," *Leadership Journal*, Christianity Today Library. http://www.ctlibrary.com/le/1984/fall/84l4032.html.

[98] John 15:5.

[99] Brother Lawrence, *The Practice of the Presence of God and the Spiritual Maxims* (New York: Cosimo Inc., 2006).

[100] Mother Teresa, We Can Do No Great Things, Only Small Things with Great Love. http://www.brainyquote.com/quotes/quotes/m/mothertere158106.html.

[101] Terry Teykl, *The Presence Based Church* (Muncie: Prayer Point Press, 2006).

[102] Jim Cymbala, "Keeping Connected to the Power," from the book *Deepening Your Ministry Through Prayer and Personal Growth*. http://www.ctlibrary.com/lebooks/libraryofchristianleadership/prayerpersonalgrowth/lclead04-12.html.

[103] John 15:4-5.

[104] Ritenbaugh, John W., "Dependence Upon God," Bible Tools. http://bibletools.org/index.cfm/fuseaction/Topical.show/RTD/cgg/ ID/681/Dependence-Upon-God.htm.

[105] Elliot, Elisabeth, "Learning to Depend on God," Back to the Bible. http://backtothebible.org/gateway-to-joy/learning-to-depend-on-god. html.

[106] 2 Chronicles 20:15, 17.

[107] 2 Chronicles 20:22.

[108] Psalms 91, 103, 23, 18, 27, 30.

[109] Dr. V. Raymond Edman, "But God," *Decision Magazine*, April 1997, 26, 27.

[110] Psalm 3:1-3 (KJV).

[111] Malachi 3:10.

[112] Hannah Whitehall Smith, Christian Quotes on Dependence on God and the Dangers of Independence. http://dailychristianquote.com/dcqdependence.html.

[113] Is. 59:2.

[114] John 3:16-18.

[115] Matthew 5:3.

[116] 2 Corinthians 12:10.

[117] 2 Corinthians 13:4.

[118] John 15:5.

[119] Bishop James R. King, sermon, St. Simon's United Methodist Church, St. Simon's Island, GA, March 22, 2009.

[120] William Gibson, *The Miracle Worker*, television adaptation, 2000.

[121] Ben Patterson, "Long Obedience" from the book *Deepening Your Conversation with God: Learning to Love to Pray*, (Bloomington: Bethany House, 1999). Christianity Today Library, http://www.ctlibrary.com/lebooks/thepastorssoul/soulconversation/pstsoul7-7.html.

[122] Randy Pausch and Jeffrey Zaslow, *The Last Lecture*, (New York: Hyperion, 2008).

[123] Philippians 4:13.

[124] John Hesselink, "The Word Did It," Christianity Today Library, July 1, 1981. http://www.ctlibrary.com/le/1981/summer/8113034.html.

[125] Luke 18:1-8.

[126] Jimmy Swaggart Ministries, television program, April 15, 2009.

[127] Dr. Bob Benson and Michael W. Benson, *Disciplines for the Inner Life* (Nashville: Thomas Nelson Inc., 1989), 197.

[128] Joshua L. Liebman, *Peace of Mind* (New York: Simon and Schuster, 1946).

[129] Peace Pilgrim, "Steps Toward Inner Peace," KPFK radio, Los Angeles, CA. http://www.peacepilgrim.com/steps1.htm.

[130] Id.

[131] Howard H. Brinton, *The Quaker Doctrine of Inward Peace* (Whitefish: Kessinger Publishing, 1960).

[132] Id, 9-10.

[133] Id., citing Job Scott's Journal, 43.

[134] Id., 18-21.

[135] John 14:27.

[136] Charles L. Allen, *Life More Abundant* (Old Tappan: Fleming H. Reville Co., 1968), 121.

[137] 1 John 1:9.

[138] Matthew 6:14.

[139] Allen, 123.

[140] I Kings 19:11-12.

[141] I Kings 19:12-13.

[142] Psalm 46:10.

[143] Romans 8:28.

[144] Matthew 14:21 tells us there were about 5,000 men alone, not including women and children.

[145] Matthew 14:20.

[146] Robert A. Emmons and Michael E. McCullough, "Counting Blessings versus Burdens: An Experimental Investigation of Gratitude and Subjective Well-Being in Daily Life," the *Journal of Personality and Social Psychology*, 2003, Vol. 84 No. 2, 377-389.

[147] Jerry Lopper, "Gratitude Improves Your Health, How to Be Healthy with Gratitude", May 24, 2006. http://personaldevelopment.suite101.com/article.cfm/gratitude_and_your_health.

[148] The study by Doctors Emmons and McCullough would appear to contradict the temporary fix argument.

[149] The study by Doctors Emmons and McCullough, however, would appear to contradict the "temporary fix" argument.

[150] Philippians 4:11.

[151] Steve Pavlina, "Gratitude," January 22, 2007. www.stevepavlina.com.

[152] Id.

[153] Genesis 50:20.

[154] Romans 8:28.

[155] Chuck Gallozzi, "Showing Gratitude." http://www.personal-development.com/chuck/gratitude.htm.

[156] John 2:1-10.

[157] Michael Zigarelli, "Restoring Joy to Your Life". www.christianitytoday.com/workplace/articles/issue15-restoringjoytoyourlife.html, 1.

[158] Matthew 5:12.

[159] Jone Johnson Lewis, Wisdom Quotes: Quotations to Inspire and Challenge. http://www.wisdomquotes.com/cat_joy.html.

[160] Dale Carnegie, *How to Stop Worrying and Start Living*, (New York: Simon & Schuster, Inc., 1944), 146.

[161] Zigarelli, p. 6.

[162] Earl Palmer, "Joy: Spiritual Health Made Visible." http://www.christianitytoday.com/le/1998/fall/8l4035.html.

[163] Id.

[164] Habakkuk 3:17-19.

[165] Ginger Kolbaba, "Unearthing Joy," *Today's Christian Woman*, November/December, 2008.

[166] John 16:33.

[167] Palmer, p.3.